National Curriculum Standards for Social Studies

I Culture

Social studies programs should include experiences that provide for the study of culture and cultural diversity.

II Time, Continuity, & Change

Social studies programs should include experiences that provide for the study of the ways human beings view themselves in and over time while recognizing examples of change and cause and effect relationships.

III People, Places, & Environments

Social studies programs should include experiences that provide for the study of people, places, and environments.

IV Individual Development & Identity

Social studies programs should include experiences that provide for the study of individual development and identity while recognizing personal changes over time and personal connections to places.

V Individuals, Groups, & Institutions

Social studies programs should include experiences that provide for the study of interactions among individuals, groups, and institutions while giving examples of and explaining, group and institutional influences on people, events, and elements of culture.

VI Power, Authority, & Governance

Social studies programs should include experiences that provide for the study of how people create and change structures of power, authority, and governance while examining the rights and responsibilities of the individual in relation to his or her social group.

VII Production, Distribution, & Consumption

Social studies programs should include experiences that provide for the study of how people organize for the production, distribution, and consumption of goods and services.

VIII Science, Technology, & Society

Social studies programs should include experiences that provide for the study of relationships among science, technology, and society.

IX Global Connections

Social studies programs should include experiences that provide for the study of global connections and independence while giving examples of conflict, cooperation, and interdependence among individuals, groups, and nations.

X Civic Ideals & Practices

Social studies programs should include experiences that provide for the study of the ideals, principles, and practices of citizenship in a democratic republic.

National Geography Standards

The *Geographically Informed Person* knows and understands . . .

THE WORLD IN SPATIAL TERMS

STANDARD 1:   How to use maps and other geographic representations, tools, and technologies to acquire, process, and report information.

STANDARD 2:   How to use mental maps to organize information about people, places, and environments.

STANDARD 3:   How to analyze the spatial organization of people, places, and environments on Earth's surface.

PLACES AND REGIONS

STANDARD 4:   The physical and human characteristics of places.

STANDARD 5:   That people create regions to interpret Earth's complexity.

STANDARD 6:   How culture and experience influence people's perception of places and regions.

PHYSICAL SYSTEMS

STANDARD 7:   The physical processes that shape the patterns of Earth's surface.

STANDARD 8:   The characteristics and spatial distribution of ecosystems on Earth's surface.

HUMAN SYSTEMS

STANDARD 9:   The characteristics, distribution, and migration of human populations on Earth's surface.

STANDARD 10: The characteristics, distributions, and complexity of Earth's cultural mosaics.

STANDARD 11: The patterns and networks of economic interdependence on Earth's surface.

STANDARD 12: The process, patterns, and functions of human settlement.

STANDARD 13: How forces of cooperation and conflict among people influence the division and control of Earth's surface.

ENVIRONMENT AND SOCIETY

STANDARD 14: How human actions modify the physical environment.

STANDARD 15: How physical systems affect human systems.

STANDARD 16: The changes that occur in the meaning, use, distribution, and importance of resources.

THE USES OF GEOGRAPHY

STANDARD 17: How to apply geography to interpret the past.

STANDARD 18: To apply geography to interpret the present and plan for the future.

Macmillan/McGraw-Hill TIMELINKS

The United States

PROGRAM AUTHORS

James A. Banks
Kevin P. Colleary
Linda Greenow
Walter C. Parker
Emily M. Schell
Dinah Zike

CONTRIBUTORS

Raymond C. Jones
Irma M. Olmedo

Mc Graw Hill **Macmillan/McGraw-Hill**

Volume 2

PROGRAM AUTHORS

James A. Banks, Ph.D.
Kerry and Linda Killinger
  Professor of Diversity Studies
  and Director, Center for
  Multicultural Education
University of Washington
Seattle, Washington

Kevin P. Colleary, Ed.D.
Curriculum and Teaching Department
Graduate School of Education
Fordham University
New York, New York

Linda Greenow, Ph.D.
Associate Professor and Chair
Department of Geography
State University of New York at
  New Paltz
New Paltz, New York

Walter C. Parker, Ph.D.
Professor of Social Studies Education
University of Washington
Seattle, Washington

Emily M. Schell, Ed.D.
Visiting Professor,
Teacher Education
San Diego State University
San Diego, California

Dinah Zike
Educational Consultant
Dinah-Mite Activities, Inc.
San Antonio, Texas

CONTRIBUTORS

Raymond C. Jones, Ph.D.
Director of Secondary Social Studies
  Education
Wake Forest University
Winston-Salem, North Carolina

Irma M. Olmedo
Associate Professor
University of Illinois-Chicago
College of Education
Chicago, Illinois

HISTORIANS/SCHOLARS

Rabbi Pamela Barmash, Ph.D.
Associate Professor of Hebrew Bible
  and Biblical Hebrew and Director,
  Program in Jewish, Islamic and Near
  Eastern Studies
Washington University
St. Louis, Missouri

Thomas Bender, Ph.D.
Professor of History
New York University,
New York, New York

Ned Blackhawk
Associate Professor of History and
  American Indian Studies
University of Wisconsin
Madison, Wisconsin

Chun-shu Chang
Professor of History
University of Michigan
Ann Arbor, Michigan

Manuel Chavez, Ph.D.
Associate Director, Center for Latin
  American & Caribbean Studies,
  Assistant Professor, School of
  Journalism
Michigan State University
East Lansing, Michigan

Sheilah F. Clarke-Ekong, Ph.D.
Professor of Anthropology
University of Missouri-St. Louis
St. Louis, Missouri

Lawrence Dale, Ph.D.
Director, Center for Economic
  Education
Arkansas State University
Jonesboro, Arkansas

Mac Dixon-Fyle, Ph.D.
Professor of History
DePauw University
Greencastle, Indiana

Carl W. Ernst
William R. Kenan, Jr., Distinguished
  Professor
Department of Religious Studies
Director, Carolina Center for the
  Study of the Middle East and Muslim
  Civilizations
University of North Carolina
Chapel Hill, North Carolina

Brooks Green, Ph.D.
Associate Professor of Geography
University of Central Arkansas
Conway, Arkansas

Sumit Guha, Ph.D.
Professor of History
Rutgers
The State University of New Jersey
New Brunswick, New Jersey

Thomas C. Holt, Ph.D.
Professor of History
University of Chicago
Chicago, Illinois

Richard E. Keady, Ph.D.
Professor, Comparative Religious
  Studies
San Jose State University
San Jose, California

The **McGraw·Hill** Companies

**Macmillan
McGraw-Hill**

Send all inquires to:

Macmillan/McGraw-Hill
8787 Orion Place
Columbus, OH 43240-4027

MHID 0-02-152405-X

ISBN 978-0-02-152405-1

Printed in the United States of America.

3 4 5 6 7 8 9 10   071/043   13 12 11 10 09

The United States

CONTENTS, Volume 2

EXPLORE The Big Idea What causes a society to grow?

How does a nation protect its freedoms?

Reference Section

Skills and Features

Maps

The New Nation

EXPLORE The Big Idea

Essential Question
What causes a society to grow?

FOLDABLES Study Organizer

Draw Conclusions
Make and label a Four-tab envelope Foldable before you read Unit 5. Label the four tabs: **New Lands, Population Changes, New Inventions,** and **New Methods of Transportation.** Use the Foldable to organize information as you read.

LOG ON
For more about Unit 5 go to www.macmillanmh.com

PEOPLE, PLACES, AND EVENTS

James Madison

Tecumseh

Philadelphia

1787
James Madison helps to create the United States Constitution.

Indiana Territory

1811
Tecumseh's forces are defeated at the Battle of Tippecanoe.

1780

1795

1810

In 1787 **James Madison** helped to create the United States **Constitution**, our nation's plan for government.

Today you can see the U.S. Constitution on display in Washington, D.C.

In 1811 Native Americans, led by **Tecumseh**, were defeated at the **Battle of Tippecanoe**.

Today in Ohio a play is performed every summer that tells the story of Tecumseh's life.

LOG ON

For more about People, Places, and Events, visit
www.macmillanmh.com

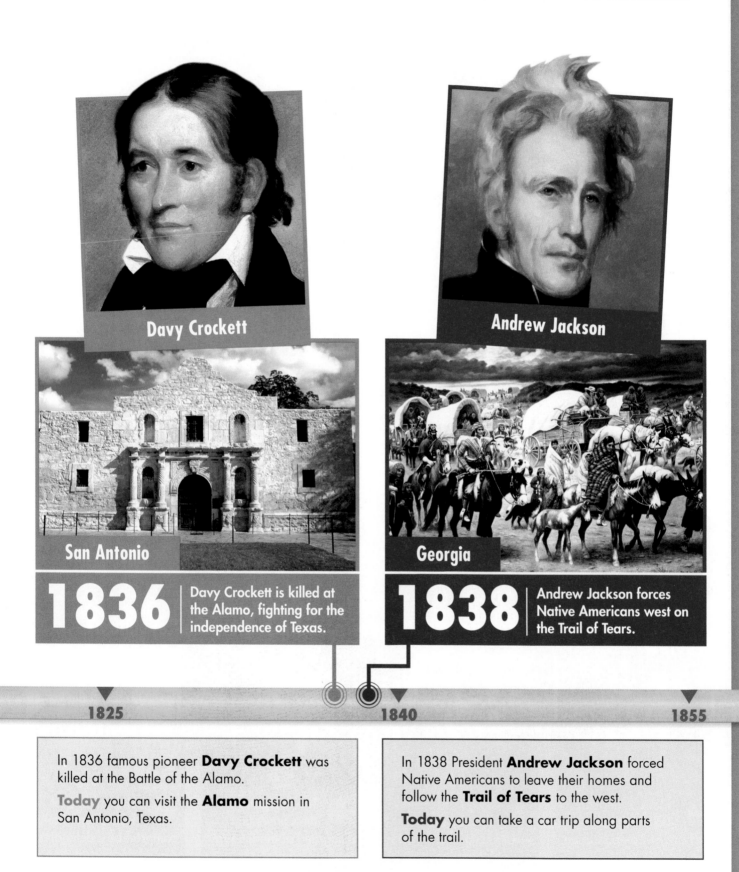

Davy Crockett

Andrew Jackson

San Antonio

Georgia

1836 Davy Crockett is killed at the Alamo, fighting for the independence of Texas.

1838 Andrew Jackson forces Native Americans west on the Trail of Tears.

1825

1840

1855

In 1836 famous pioneer **Davy Crockett** was killed at the Battle of the Alamo.

Today you can visit the **Alamo** mission in San Antonio, Texas.

In 1838 President **Andrew Jackson** forced Native Americans to leave their homes and follow the **Trail of Tears** to the west.

Today you can take a car trip along parts of the trail.

Planning a New Government

VOCABULARY

Articles of Confederation p. 197

arsenal p. 198

legislature p. 200

READING SKILL

Draw Conclusions

Copy the chart below. Use it to draw conclusions about the need for a new plan for government.

Text Clues	Conclusion

STANDARDS FOCUS

SOCIAL STUDIES   Global Connections

GEOGRAPHY   The World in Spatial Terms

During the hot summer of 1787, delegates argued about a new plan for American government.

Visual Preview

What problems did the government face after the Revolution?

A Many Americans believed that the Articles of Confederation were a failure.

B Shays's Rebellion showed the weakness of the Articles of Confederation.

C The delegates at the Convention disagreed about the way to share power.

D After months of debate and many compromises, delegates signed the Constitution.

Ⓐ THE ARTICLES OF CONFEDERATION

Every government needs a plan. In 1777 the Second Continental Congress approved the **Articles of Confederation**—*the first plan of government for the United States.*

At first, the Articles of Confederation met the needs of the young nation. But its weaknesses soon became obvious.

No Central Government

Under the Articles of Confederation, each state was independent. Each state printed its own money and passed its own trade laws. Money changed value between states. Merchants were uncertain which trade laws to follow.

Under the Articles of Confederation, the national government could not collect taxes. It had to ask the states for money. Congress needed money to pay off its large debts. The government also could not pay lawmakers. Even worse, it couldn't pay soldiers who had served in the Revolution.

Plan for Settlement

Overall, the articles didn't work. One law passed by Congress *did* work. The Ordinance of 1787 (also called the Northwest Ordinance) was a plan for land north of the Ohio River and east of the Mississippi River. This region was known as the Northwest Territory. The Ordinance stated that an area became a territory when its population reached 5,000. It could apply for statehood when the population reached 60,000. The states of Ohio, Indiana, Illinois, Michigan, and Wisconsin were settled this way. The Northwest Ordinance also pushed Native Americans off their land. As a result, battles between settlers and Native Americans soon broke out.

QUICK CHECK

Draw Conclusions **Why did settlers and Native Americans battle in the Northwest Territories?**

The Northwest Territory, 1787

Map Skill

LOCATION **Why was the area on the map known as the Northwest Territory?**

REBELLION IN MASSACHUSETTS

In 1786 the weaknesses of the Articles of Confederation led to violence in western Massachusetts. To raise money to pay state debts, Massachusetts lawmakers raised taxes on property. Lawmakers also said that people had to pay their taxes in gold or silver. The state's paper currency had little value—and there was no national currency.

Most farmers in western Massachusetts were in debt. When the legislature refused to accept paper money, hundreds of farmers were unable to pay their taxes. Those who could not pay often lost their farms. Many landed in jail.

Farmers Fight Back

To many farmers, Massachusetts lawmakers were no better than the British Parliament. Many farmers had fought the British, and had been paid in worthless paper money. Daniel Shays, a farmer who was once a Patriot officer, urged others to rebel. Shays led his men, called Regulators, across western Massachusetts. They closed courthouses and broke into jails to

free debtors. News of what became known as Shays's Rebellion spread quickly.

Massachusetts leaders asked Congress to send regular army troops to capture Shays. The government had no power to raise money to pay troops. Instead, the state's governor and wealthy lawmakers paid for a private militia force with their own money.

In January 1787, more than 1,000 farmers attacked a state **arsenal**—a storage place for weapons—in Springfield, Massachusetts. There they were met by the private militia, which had better weapons, including a cannon. Cannon fire killed four rebels and wounded twenty. Many rebel farmers were captured, and some were sentenced to death. Shays finally fled to New York.

▼ Regulators blocked courthouses during Shays's Rebellion.

▼ Paper money was the only money most farmers had to pay their taxes.

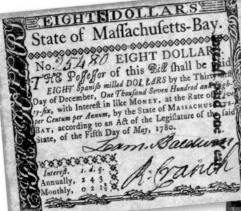

The Meaning of Shays's Rebellion

Shays's Rebellion showed Americans, both rich and poor, that the Articles of Confederation had failed. Wealthy Americans wanted a national government strong enough to protect their property. Farmers wanted a government with the power to issue paper money that had value.

James Madison, whom you will soon read about, called for a meeting to decide on a new plan for government. Madison believed that unless the plan for government was changed, trouble would continue. The United States needed a plan that joined the states together under a central government that had power to pass laws for all Americans. He wrote:

> **The rebellion in Massachusetts is a warning.**

QUICK CHECK

Draw Conclusions Why did Madison call Shays's Rebellion a "warning"?

Shays's "Regulators" attacked an arsenal in Springfield, Massachusetts. A private militia hired by business owners defeated Shays's men.

MEETING IN PHILADELPHIA

How would you like to spend the summer shut inside a room? Delegates who created the plan for our nation's government did this when they met in Philadelphia on May 25, 1787. The delegates remained in hot rooms for almost four months. This meeting was called the Constitutional Convention.

A Difficult Task

Some delegates, such as Benjamin Franklin and George Washington, were well known. The most important delegate, however, stood 5 feet 4 inches tall and weighed 100 pounds—James Madison from Virginia. Madison believed that the Articles of Confederation had failed. He also knew that creating a new plan for government would be difficult. He wrote:

❝In framing a government . . . the great difficulty lies in this: you must first enable the government to control the governed, and in the next place, oblige [force] it to control itself.❞

Two Different Plans

Today, we often think of the President as the most important person in government. But in 1787, the **legislature** was the most important part of government. A legislature is an elected body of people that make the laws. Madison's plan, the Virginia Plan, created a national legislature with two "houses." One house would be elected by citizens. In those days, only white men with property were allowed to

Delegates met in this room to argue about the new plan for government. James Madison later wrote, "Every word of the Constitution decides a question between power and liberty."

vote. The members of the second house would be chosen by the members of the first house. The number of members in the first house was based on a state's population. This meant that the largest states had the most representatives.

James Madison is called the "Father of the Constitution."

It is no surprise that delegates from small states disliked Madison's plan. Under the Articles of Confederation all states had equal power. William Paterson, a delegate from New Jersey, offered his New Jersey Plan—a legislature with only one house in which each state would have one vote.

Delegates argued for weeks during the heat of summer. Madison continued to support the Virginia Plan. He believed that it was more important to reach an agreement that satisfied everyone. He led the discussions that tried to find a way for states to share power.

QUICK CHECK

Draw Conclusions **Why did Madison believe that creating a new plan for government would be difficult?**

IMPORTANT COMPROMISES

After months of disagreement, Roger Sherman, a delegate from the small state of Connecticut, introduced a plan that solved the biggest problem facing the convention.

States Share Power

Under Sherman's plan, the legislature would have a House of Representatives, with the number of representatives based on a state's population. That pleased large states. In the Senate, each state would have two Senators. That pleased small states.

Under Sherman's plan, representatives would serve two years and be elected directly by the people. Senators would serve six-year terms and be chosen by state legislatures. A law would pass only when both houses approved it. Sherman's plan became known as the Great Compromise. Years later, laws changed to allow the people to elect Senators directly.

The Constitutional Convention was held in Independence Hall in Philadelphia. ▼

The Issue of Slavery

Almost half the delegates at the convention owned enslaved workers. These delegates wanted the workers to count as part of the population. Many delegates disagreed—thinking that would give too much power to states with enslaved people. So delegates reached the Three-Fifths Compromise. Every five enslaved people counted as three free people.

A Plan for Voting

Delegates wanted the United States to have a President. If Congress made the choice, as Madison suggested, the President would serve lawmakers rather than the American people. Instead, the delegates created

Population of the 13 States, 1790

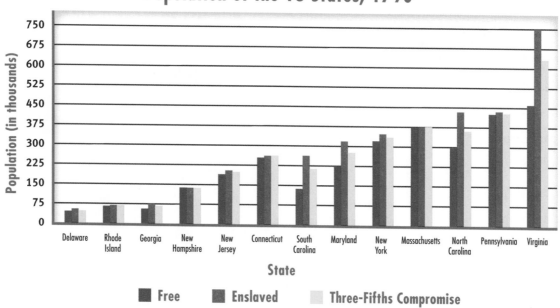

Population (in thousands) vs **State**

Legend: ■ Free ■ Enslaved ▫ Three-Fifths Compromise

the Electoral College. In the Electoral College, the number of electoral votes for each state was based on the number of its Congressional representatives. The electoral votes would then be cast for the candidate chosen by the people in their states.

The Signing

Finally, after nearly four months, the 39 delegates signed the Constitution on September 17, 1787. It had been a struggle to reach an agreement. In the end, with Madison leading the way, they created the United States Constitution. Today, James Madison is known as the "Father of the Constitution."

QUICK CHECK

Draw Conclusions **Why is James Madison called the "Father of the Constitution"?**

◄ Roger Sherman of Connecticut offered a plan for sharing power between large and small states.

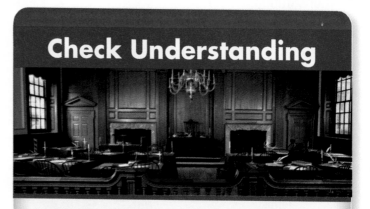

Check Understanding

1. **VOCABULARY** Describe the problems of the early government using these terms.

   Articles of Confederation

   legislature

2. **READING SKILL** Draw Conclusions Use the chart from page 196 to explain why delegates opposed Madison's idea for electing the President.

Text Clues	Conclusion

 EXPLORE The Big Idea 3. **Write About It** Explain how the Constitution helped large and small states grow together as a nation.

Lesson 2

United States Constitution

VOCABULARY

federal system p. 205

Supreme Court p. 205

ratify p. 208

bill of rights p. 208

amendment p. 209

READING SKILL

Draw Conclusions

Copy the chart below. Use it to draw conclusions about the United States Constitution.

Text Clues	Conclusion

STANDARDS FOCUS

SOCIAL STUDIES   Global Connection

GEOGRAPHY   The World in Spatial Terms

The ratification of the United States Constitution was celebrated with a parade in New York City.

Visual Preview

Why is the Constitution a powerful document?

A State and national governments share power under the Constitution.

B The Constitution has a system of checks and balances for sharing power.

C Anti-federalists wanted a bill of rights before they would ratify the Constitution.

D Advisors worked with George Washington, the first President.

Ⓐ POWER OF GOVERNMENT

The first three words of the United States Constitution explain a great deal about the government of the United States. These words are: "We the People . . ."

The delegates to the Constitutional Convention agreed that both state and national governments should share powers. This is known as a **federal system**. Under a federal system, national and state governments both make laws and collect taxes. State governments, however, control local matters, such as police services and public education.

After the Preamble, which you can read on this page, the Constitution is divided into separate parts called articles. The first three articles explain how the United States government is organized.

Article 1 establishes a legislature, called Congress, made up of a Senate and a House of Representatives. This branch has the power to make laws. Article 2 creates the office of the President, the leader of the Executive Branch, to enforce the laws. Article 3 establishes a Supreme Court. The **Supreme Court** is the highest court in the United States. It has the power to decide whether any laws work against the Constitution.

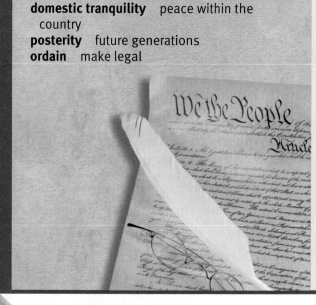

Primary Sources

We the People of the United States, in Order to form a more perfect Union, establish Justice, insure **domestic Tranquility**, provide for the common Defense, promote the general Welfare, and secure the Blessings of Liberty to ourselves and our **Posterity,** do **ordain** and establish this constitution for the United States of America.

Preamble to the Constitution of the United States approved by the states in 1788

domestic tranquility   peace within the country
posterity   future generations
ordain   make legal

QUICK CHECK

Draw Conclusions Why did delegates want state and national governments to share power?

Write About It Rewrite the Preamble after "We the People" in your own words.

Checks and Balances

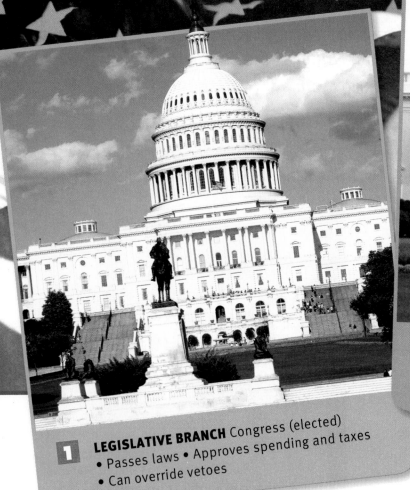

2 **EXECUTIVE BRANCH** President (elected)
• Enforces laws • Commander-in-Chief of military • Signs or vetoes laws

1 **LEGISLATIVE BRANCH** Congress (elected)
• Passes laws • Approves spending and taxes
• Can override vetoes

B BALANCE OF POWER

Many delegates to the Constitutional Convention had fought in the American Revolution to free the colonies from King George III and the British Parliament. They wanted to make certain that no branch of the United States government could become as powerful as the king or British lawmakers. That is why they created a system of government under the Constitution that gave each branch the power to check, or stop, the work of another branch.

Checks and Balances

The system of keeping one branch from gaining too much power is known as checks and balances. In the legislative branch, there are checks between the two houses. Congress can pass legislation only if both the House of Representatives and the Senate pass exactly the same measure.

There are checks between branches as well. For a measure to become law, the President must sign it. The President is also allowed to

3 JUDICIAL BRANCH Supreme Court and federal courts (appointed) • Decides Constitutional questions about laws

Write About It In your opinion, which branch is the most important part of government? Explain.

veto, or reject, a law. Congress can override, or cancel, the President's veto with a two-thirds vote in each house.

In the judicial branch, the Supreme Court has the power to declare a law unconstitutional. This power, known as judicial review, was first used in the case of *Marbury* v. *Madison* in 1803.

The powers of the three branches of government are also balanced. Under the Constitution, no branch can take the powers given to another branch. The President cannot decide whether laws are constitutional.

Congress cannot enforce laws. The Supreme Court cannot make laws. Some delegates complained that the new Constitution created too strong a plan for government. But James Madison defended the system of checks and balances. He wrote:

> **"If men were angels, no government would be necessary."**

QUICK CHECK

Draw Conclusions Why did delegates believe that power should be shared among the three branches?

At least nine of the thirteen states had to **ratify**, or officially approve, the Constitution. Supporters of the Constitution called themselves Federalists. Those opposing the Constitution, the Anti-federalists, wanted a more limited plan for federal government, such as that created by the Articles of Confederation.

Debate Over the Constitution

Federalists took steps to explain the advantages of the new Constitution. Their explanations appeared in a series of 85 newspaper essays written by Alexander Hamilton, James Madison, and John Jay. These essays are now known as *The Federalist Papers*.

Anti-federalists also spoke out. In Virginia, George Mason, who had been a delegate at the Philadelphia convention, wrote:

"There is no declaration of any kind, for preserving the liberty of the press, or the trial by jury . . . ."

Mason and many others agreed that the Constitution needed a **bill of rights**. This was a statement of the liberties guaranteed by the government to the people. Many state constitutions already had a bill of rights. For that reason, Madison and Hamilton argued that a bill of rights was not necessary in the United States Constitution.

Ratification

In June 1788 the Constitution officially became the law of the United States when New Hampshire became the ninth state to ratify it. Two of the largest states, Virginia and New York, had strong groups of Anti-

❧ Bill of Rights ❧

First Ten Amendments

First	People have freedom of religion, freedom of speech, freedom of the press; the right to assemble peacefully; the right to complain about government
Second	People have the right to own and use firearms
Third	Prevents the government from forcing people to house soldiers during peacetime
Fourth	People cannot be searched or have property taken without reason
Fifth	Protects people who are accused of crimes
Sixth	Guarantees the right to trial by jury and a lawyer in criminal cases
Seventh	Guarantees the right to trial by jury in civil cases
Eighth	Prohibits high bail, fines, and cruel or unusual punishment
Ninth	The rights of the people are not limited to those in the Constitution
Tenth	Powers not given to the federal government belong to the states or to the people

Alexander Hamilton
was a key figure in the founding of the United States. He was a Patriot officer in the Revolution as a teenager. After the war, he became a strong Federalist. Hamilton became the first Secretary of the Treasury under George Washington.

Alexander Hamilton

federalists who fought against ratification. They demanded that the Constitution spell out clearly the rights of the people. A nation that had won independence from a king would never approve a plan that did not guarantee their liberties, said the Anti-federalists. Federalists such as Virginia's Madison and New York's Hamilton believed that without ratification by large states, the Constitution, and the federal government, would be weak.

Adding the Bill of Rights

To win ratification of the large states, Madison agreed to submit a bill of rights to Congress for approval. He promised Anti-federalists that he would work to get the bill of rights approved if they voted to ratify the Constitution. Madison kept his promise. In June 1789 he asked the House of Representatives to add a bill of rights to the Constitution. Changes to the Constitution are known as **amendments**. One of the first acts of the first Congress was to pass the ten amendments known as the Bill of Rights. By 1790 all of the original 13 states had ratified the Constitution.

Changing the Constitution

Since 1790 the Constitution has had 17 other amendments added to it. To become part of the Constitution, an amendment must be approved by two-thirds of the House and Senate and then by three-fourths of the states. An amendment can also be considered if two-thirds of the states ask Congress to meet in a special session.

QUICK CHECK

Draw Conclusions Why did Anti-federalists want a bill of rights?

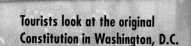

Tourists look at the original Constitution in Washington, D.C.

THE FIRST PRESIDENT

Many men and women had given their lives for liberty. Many others had done the hard work of creating a new plan of government. When it came time to elect the first President, however, there was only one choice. He had been called "The Father of the Country" by many. For once, all Americans agreed that the new nation under the new Constitution should be led by one man: George Washington.

George Washington took the oath of office as the first President in New York City.

President's Advisers

To help the President run the Executive Branch of the government, Congress created the departments of treasury, state, and war. An official called a secretary headed each office. The Secretary of the Treasury, Alexander Hamilton, formed a plan for the economy. The Secretary of State, Thomas Jefferson, handled affairs with other countries. The Secretary of War, Henry Knox, took charge of the country's defense. These advisers became known as the President's cabinet. Washington chose John Jay as the first Chief Justice, or head judge, of the U.S. Supreme Court.

In 1797 Washington returned to Mount Vernon, his plantation in Virginia, after serving two terms as President. He died two years later. Henry Lee, a representative from Virginia, expressed the feelings of many Americans when he said Washington was:

"first in war, first in peace, and first in the hearts of his countrymen."

QUICK CHECK

Draw Conclusions **Why did Lee say Washington was first in the hearts of his countrymen?**

Benjamin Banneker

Black Heritage USA 15c

◀ Benjamin Banneker laid out the streets of Washington, D.C.

A New Capital

- In 1790 government leaders decided that the capital would be moved to land along the Potomac River. Maryland and Virginia both gave land to form a new area called the District of Columbia.

- President Washington appointed Benjamin Banneker to lay out the streets of the new capital. Banneker was one of the first African Americans to work for the federal government.

Check Understanding

1. **VOCABULARY** Write a paragraph about the United States Constitution using these terms.

   federal system   **amendment**
   Bill of Rights

2. **READING SKILL** Draw Conclusions Use the chart from page 204 to write a paragraph about James Madison.

Text Clues	Conclusion

3. **Write About It** Write about how the Bill of Rights helped to shape American society.

Lesson 3

VOCABULARY

pioneer p. 213

impressment p. 215

READING SKILL

Draw Conclusions
Copy the chart below. As you read, use it to draw a conclusion about the Corps of Discovery.

Text Clues	Conclusion

STANDARDS FOCUS

SOCIAL STUDIES Individuals, Groups, and Institutions

GEOGRAPHY World in Spatial Terms

Lewis and Clark explored the Missouri River and western lands.

Visual Preview

How did the expansion of the United States affect North America?

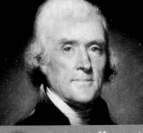

A During Jefferson's term, Congress bought the Louisiana Territory.

B Lewis and Clark's team explored the Louisiana Territory, and Jefferson avoided war.

A OPENING THE WEST

By a crackling fire, John Findley told his old friend Daniel Boone about an incredible place of huge buffalo herds, deer at every salt lick, and rich farmland. He had seen Kentucky from the Ohio River. Now he needed an overland route that a wagon could pass through.

Daniel Boone and John Findley found a passage through the Appalachian Mountains that they called the Cumberland Gap. Working with other men, Boone carved a road wide enough for wagons that was called the Wilderness Road. It became the main route for Americans going west in the late 1700s.

The first people to enter a region are called **pioneers**. White settlers called themselves pioneers. The area west of the Appalachians had been home to Native Americans for centuries. In the 1790s, Native American groups joined together to drive white settlers off their lands.

President Washington sent the army to Ohio three times to protect settlers. In 1794 American soldiers defeated Native Americans at the Battle of Fallen Timbers in Ohio. The next year, some Native American leaders there accepted the Treaty of Greenville. Other leaders refused to sign the treaty. They did not want to lose their lands. Trouble between settlers and Native Americans continued into the 1800s.

French Louisiana

In the South, the French port city of New Orleans had become important to the growing trade of the western territories along the Mississippi River. In 1803 American representatives in France offered to buy New Orleans for $10 million. At the same time, the French needed to pay for a war against Great Britain. To the surprise of Americans, the French offered to sell the entire Louisiana Territory for $15 million. Congress agreed to the price. The purchase nearly doubled the size of the United States.

QUICK CHECK

Draw Conclusions **How do you think Native Americans who refused to sign the Treaty of Greenville felt about pioneers?**

EVENT

In the **election of 1800,** Thomas Jefferson led a new party called the Democratic-Republicans to a hard-fought victory. The election led to a case in which the Supreme Court claimed the right to decide whether laws were constitutional.

Election of 1800

THE LOUISIANA TERRITORY

The United States got a tremendous bargain—almost 525 million acres of land for about 3 cents an acre. But few Americans knew anything about this huge territory. Some believed that woolly mammoths roamed the land and that the Native Americans spoke Welsh. Others believed the Northwest Passage lay within the territory.

Lewis and Clark

President Jefferson chose Meriwether Lewis, his secretary, to lead what is called the Corps of Discovery. In June 1803, Lewis offered to share command with his army officer friend, William Clark. He was the younger brother of George Rogers Clark, the Revolutionary War hero.

The expedition set out to map the course of the Missouri River and find a land route to the Pacific Ocean. Jefferson also wanted information about the land, its resources, and the Native Americans who lived in the region. It was a journey that would take them thousands of miles. They would see lands, rivers, and people that no white American had seen before.

In May 1804, the Corps of Discovery headed west from St. Louis on the Missouri River. William Clark relied on a compass to measure land distances, directions, and

◄ Meriwether Lewis (left) and William Clark (right)

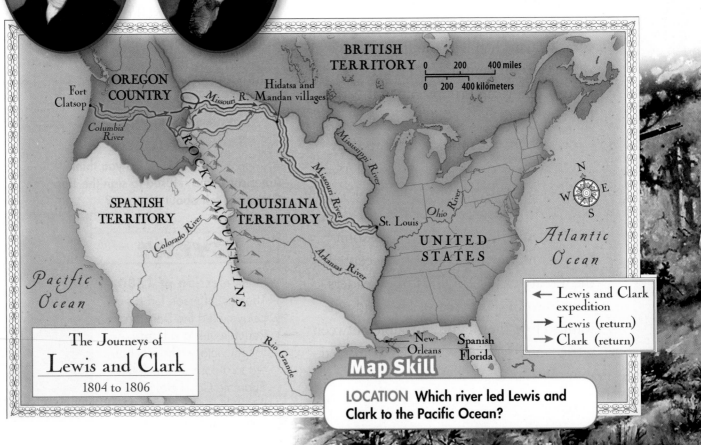

The Journeys of **Lewis and Clark**
1804 to 1806

Map Skill

LOCATION **Which river led Lewis and Clark to the Pacific Ocean?**

landforms. Other instruments used to survey and map the land were a quadrant, sextant, and chronometer.

In 1805 the group was joined by a Shoshone woman named Sacagawea, who served as a guide and interpreter. Sacagawea traveled with the expedition to the Pacific Ocean and back. Lewis and Clark traveled 8,000 miles, mostly on Native American trails, following Native American maps, and led by Native American guides. They returned to St. Louis in 1806.

Jefferson's Foreign Policy

During Jefferson's term in office, France and Great Britain were at war. The United States did not take sides in this war. Americans continued to trade with both countries. This enraged both the British and the French. Warships from both countries stopped American merchant ships at sea and took their goods. The British also forced American sailors to serve on British ships. This practice, called **impressment**, enraged Americans.

To protect American ships and lives, an angry Congress passed the Embargo Act in 1807. The act closed all American ports. No ships could trade in American waters. This law was a bad idea. It was passed to hurt Great Britain and France. Instead, it hurt American shipping and weakened the nation's economy. In spite of efforts to avoid conflict, relations with France and Great Britain grew worse. The United States was at the edge of war.

QUICK CHECK

Draw Conclusions **Why would closing American ports weaken the nation's economy?**

▼ Sacagawea guided Lewis and Clark during their exploration of the Louisiana Territory.

Check Understanding

1. **VOCABULARY** Draw a picture illustrating one of these vocabulary words.

   pioneer   impressment

2. **READING SKILL** Draw Conclusions Use your chart from page 212 to help you write about the Corps of Discovery.

Text Clues	Conclusion

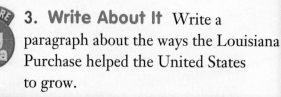

3. **Write About It** Write a paragraph about the ways the Louisiana Purchase helped the United States to grow.

Lesson 4

VOCABULARY

War Hawks p. 217

Era of Good Feelings p. 219

Adams-Onís Treaty p. 219

Monroe Doctrine p. 220

READING SKILL

Draw Conclusions
Copy the chart below. As you read, use it to draw conclusions about the War of 1812.

Text Clues	Conclusion

STANDARDS FOCUS

SOCIAL STUDIES Power, Authority, and Governance

GEOGRAPHY The Uses of Geography

The War of 1812

In the Battle of Lake Erie, the United States defeated the British.

Visual Preview

How did the War of 1812 affect Americans?

A Americans disagreed about going to war with Great Britain.

B The end of the War of 1812 united Americans and expanded the country.

C The Monroe Doctrine stopped the colonization of the Americas after the war.

A WAR WITH GREAT BRITAIN

*When the War of 1812 began, Great Britain had been fighting with France for nearly 20 years. U.S. "**War Hawks**" believed that they could conquer Canada and take control of the whole continent.*

Many **War Hawks** were settlers from areas west of the Appalachian Mountains. To fight the settlers, the Shawnee chief Tecumseh united several Western groups. In 1811 Tecumseh's forces were defeated by troops led by General William Henry Harrison at the Battle of Tippecanoe in present-day Indiana.

"Mr. Madison's War"

The War Hawks complained that the British had helped the Native Americans in the West. The War Hawks also felt the United States should fight to protect American sailors from impressment in the British navy. In June 1812 Congress, led by lawmakers who were War Hawks, declared war on Great Britain. President James Madison signed the declaration.

Not all Americans supported the war. New England merchants depended on trade with Great Britain. They wanted to settle problems peacefully. When war broke out, New Englanders called the war "Mr. Madison's War."

QUICK CHECK

Draw Conclusions **Why did War Hawks want war with Great Britain?**

Citizenship

Mobilizing Groups

Tecumseh formed a confederacy to stop Americans from taking more land from Native Americans. Mobilizing groups is one way to organize people. Movements have been used throughout history to call attention to unfair treatment and bring change. The American Indian Movement fought to improve the lives of thousands of Native Americans living on reservations. Is there a movement you want to join?

Write About It Write about a way a group could bring change in your community.

ⓑ VICTORIES AND DEFEATS

The American navy won important victories early in the war. In 1812 the U.S.S. *Constitution* defeated the British ship *Guerrière*. When British cannonballs bounced off the thick oak sides of the *Constitution*, the ship earned the nickname "Old Ironsides."

In 1813 ships under American Oliver Hazard Perry won the Battle of Lake Erie. Perry's victory forced the British to retreat into Canada. American troops then invaded Canada. They captured supplies in York, present-day Toronto, and burned the town.

The Burning of Washington, D.C.

In 1814 the British sent thousands of well-trained soldiers to invade the United States and attack Washington, D.C. The British wanted to punish the Americans for invading Canada and destroying York.

When the British soldiers landed in Maryland, the local militia fled. British troops then marched into Washington, D.C. British officers walked through the White House with muddy boots and ate dinner in President Madison's dining room. By then, the Madisons had fled. Soon, the White House, the Capitol building, and other government buildings were in flames.

As Washington lay in ashes, the British sailed up the Chesapeake Bay to attack Baltimore, Maryland. The city was protected by Fort McHenry. British warships stopped about two miles from the fort. From that distance, the warship fired rockets at the fort. These were 32-pound metal tubes filled with gunpowder, whose tips exploded when they hit a target.

▼ The American defense of Baltimore's Fort McHenry inspired Francis Scott Key to write "The Star-Spangled Banner" in 1814.

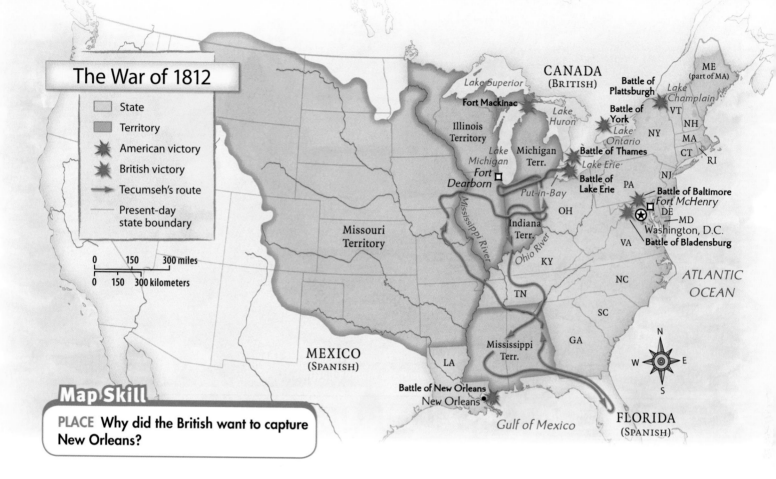

The War of 1812

- State
- Territory
- American victory
- British victory
- → Tecumseh's route
- — Present-day state boundary

0   150   300 miles
0   150   300 kilometers

CANADA (BRITISH)

Lake Superior

Fort Mackinac

Illinois Territory

Lake Huron

Battle of Plattsburgh

Lake Champlain

Battle of York

ME (part of MA)

VT

NH

NY

Lake Ontario

MA

CT

RI

Lake Michigan

Michigan Terr.

Fort Dearborn

Battle of Thames

Lake Erie

Put-in-Bay

Battle of Lake Erie

PA

NJ

OH

Indiana Terr.

Mississippi River

Ohio River

Battle of Baltimore
Fort McHenry

DE

MD

Washington, D.C.

Battle of Bladensburg

Missouri Territory

KY

VA

NC

ATLANTIC OCEAN

TN

SC

MEXICO (SPANISH)

LA

Mississippi Terr.

GA

N
W   E
S

Battle of New Orleans
New Orleans

Gulf of Mexico

FLORIDA (SPANISH)

Map Skill

PLACE Why did the British want to capture New Orleans?

The British attack on Fort McHenry began on September 13. For 25 hours, the fort was bombarded by more than 1,500 cannonballs and rockets. Francis Scott Key, an American prisoner on a British ship, watched the night sky light up with "the rockets' red glare." The next morning, Key saw that the American flag still flew over Fort McHenry. Key expressed his feelings in "The Star-Spangled Banner," a poem that later became our national anthem.

The War Ends

In December 1814, the Treaty of Ghent ended the War of 1812. Neither side won the war, but they agreed to stop fighting. News of the treaty traveled slowly. In January 1815, Americans led by Andrew Jackson crushed the British at the Battle of New Orleans. Although the treaty had been signed before this battle, Jackson became a national hero. The end of the War of 1812 created a feeling of unity among Americans. Newspapers named this period the **Era of Good Feelings**.

The United States Grows

Still a popular general, Andrew Jackson led his troops into the Spanish colony of Florida in 1818. He claimed that he was chasing Native Americans who had attacked Georgia settlements. Spain did not want to fight with Jackson or the Americans. Under the **Adams-Onís Treaty** of 1819, Spain sold Florida to the United States. In return, the United States gave up its claim to Texas west of the Sabine River.

QUICK CHECK

Draw Conclusions **Why did the British army burn Washington, D.C.?**

President James Monroe talking to his Cabinet members about the Monroe Doctrine

ⓒ THE MONROE DOCTRINE

By 1822 Spain was losing control of its colonies in the Americas. Argentina, Chile, Colombia, Mexico, and Peru had become independent countries. To prevent European countries from regaining colonies in Latin America, President James Monroe issued the **Monroe Doctrine** in 1823. It stated that the United States would not allow European powers to establish new colonies in the Americas. In return, the United States would not interfere with existing colonies in the Americas or in European affairs. The doctrine's authors saw it as a way for the United States to oppose colonial powers. Americans would later use it to expand the United States. For example, Spanish Puerto Rico became a U.S. territory in 1898.

QUICK CHECK

Draw Conclusions **Why did the United States want to prevent new European colonies in the Americas?**

Check Understanding

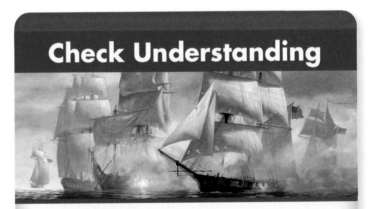

1. **VOCABULARY** Write an essay describing the relationship between Spain and the United States. Use these vocabulary terms.

   Adams-Onís Treaty   **Monroe Doctrine**

2. **READING SKILL** Draw Conclusions Use your chart from page 216 to write about the War of 1812.

Text Clues	Conclusion

3. **EXPLORE The Big Idea** **Write About It** Write about how Andrew Jackson's actions in 1818 helped the United States grow.

Map and Globe Skills

Compare Maps at Different Scales

VOCABULARY

map scale
small-scale map
large-scale map

All maps are drawn to scale. A **map scale** uses a unit of measurement, such as an inch, to show distance on Earth. A map scale explains the size of the area on a map.

A **small-scale map**, such as Map A, shows a large area, but cannot include many details. A **large-scale map**, such as Map B, shows a smaller area with more details.

Learn It

● If you want to find out where many battles occurred during the War of 1812, use a small-scale map, or Map A. It has a scale of 300 miles. It shows a large area.

● If you want to know about the Battle of Baltimore, you would need the large-scale map, or Map B. It has a scale of 2 miles and shows more details, such as ships and troop locations.

● Compare the scales of both maps.

Try It

● Which map would you use to plan a route from one state to another?

● Which map would you use to make a detailed plan of the attack on Baltimore?

Apply It

● Compare a map of the United States with a map of your state.

● Compare the map scales. Is the state map a large-scale or a small-scale map?

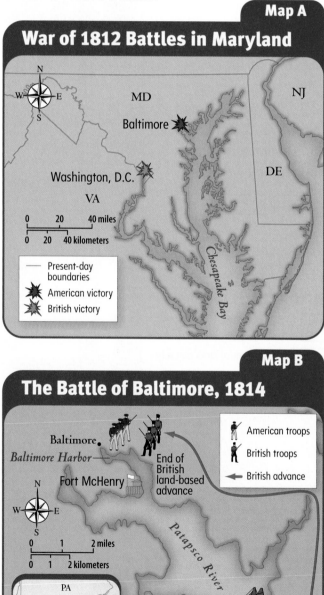

Map A

War of 1812 Battles in Maryland

MD
NJ
Baltimore
DE
Washington, D.C.
VA

0   20   40 miles
0   20   40 kilometers

Chesapeake Bay

— Present-day boundaries
✸ American victory
✸ British victory

Map B

The Battle of Baltimore, 1814

Baltimore
Baltimore Harbor
Fort McHenry
End of British land-based advance

American troops
British troops
← British advance

Patapsco River

0   1   2 miles
0   1   2 kilometers

PA
MD   NJ
WV   DE
VA

British landing

221

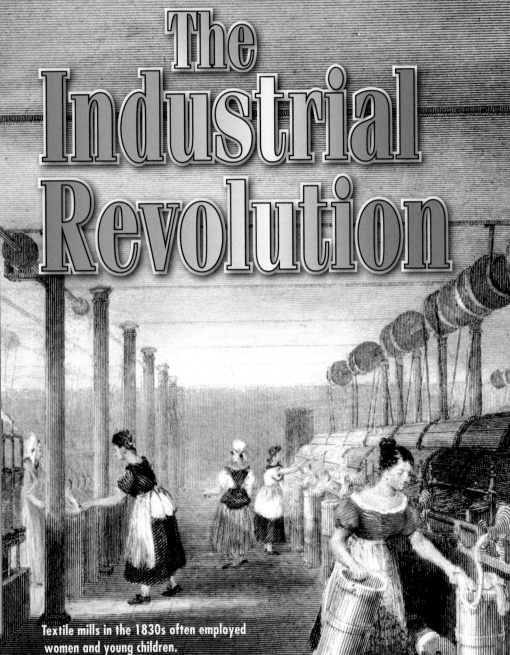

The Industrial Revolution

Lesson 5

VOCABULARY

Industrial Revolution
p. 223

cotton gin p. 223

interchangeable part
p. 223

reaper p. 224

steam engine p. 224

READING SKILL

Draw Conclusions
Copy the chart below.
As you read, draw a
conclusion about the
Industrial Revolution.

Text Clues	Conclusion

STANDARDS FOCUS

SOCIAL STUDIES Science, Technology, and Society

GEOGRAPHY Environment and Society

Textile mills in the 1830s often employed women and young children.

Visual Preview

How did the Industrial Revolution change people's lives?

A The cotton gin helped build the cotton textile industry in the United States.

B Technology impacted the way people farmed, traveled and transported goods.

Ⓐ INDUSTRY BOOMS

Until the early 1800s, most families made the items they needed, such as tools and clothes, by hand. Then came a period of rapid invention, when machines began to do the work people once did.

This period of invention was called the **Industrial Revolution**. It was a time when new machines and new ideas changed the way people worked, traveled, and lived.

The Cotton Gin

In 1793 Eli Whitney built a **cotton gin** to remove seeds from cotton. The gin, which is short for "engine," could clean more cotton in a few minutes than a whole team of workers could clean by hand in a day. The cotton gin made cotton the most important cash crop in the South.

Textile Mills

With more cotton coming from the South, textile mills grew in the North. A textile mill is a factory where workers turn cotton into cloth. In the early 1800s, mills were built near rivers because the machines were powered by water.

In 1813 Francis Cabot Lowell built a power loom at a mill in Waltham, Massachusetts. All stages of cloth-making happened in that one place. Lowell's business partners later built several textile mills, as well as a town, called Lowell, for the workers. By 1850 Lowell had more than 10,000 workers. Many were young women who left home to work in Lowell. They worked 12-hour days, six days a week, and lived on the grounds of the mill.

Whitney's Next Innovation

In 1801 Eli Whitney had another important idea—**interchangeable parts**. Interchangeable parts are pieces made in the same or standard sizes, so they would fit any specific product. A barrel for one rifle would fit another rifle of the same type, for example. With Whitney's idea, guns, tools, and other products could be made faster and at a lower cost.

QUICK CHECK

Draw Conclusions **How did mill towns change the lives of women in the 1800s?**

PLACES

Today you can visit **Lowell National Historic Park** to see the birthplace of the American Industrial Revolution. Trolleys tour the park's cotton mills and living quarters.

Lowell, Massachusetts

B CHANGES IN FARMING AND TRAVEL

Farming became much easier during the Industrial Revolution with the invention of the mechanical plow and the **reaper**. A reaper is a machine with sharp blades to cut grain. With better machines, fewer farmers were needed to raise food. As a result, many people in farming areas moved to cities to work in factories and mills.

The Steam Engine

Transportation improved quickly after the invention of the **steam engine**. Steam engines produced more power than a team of horses, and they could pull heavier loads. In 1807 Robert Fulton designed a boat powered by a steam engine. His steamboat traveled 150 miles in 32 hours. Boats without steam engines took 4 days to make the same trip.

The Erie Canal

In 1817 DeWitt Clinton, the governor of New York, began building a 363-mile canal, or human-made waterway. At that time, most canals were only a few miles long. The Erie Canal would connect Lake Erie to the Hudson River. It used a system of locks to raise and lower the water level, as shown below.

Even though people didn't believe the canal would work, construction began. Immigrants did most of the digging. The Erie Canal opened in 1825 and quickly became a success. New York City soon became the country's largest and most important port. For a few years, the Erie Canal was important to the U.S. economy. Then a new steam-powered invention made canals less important.

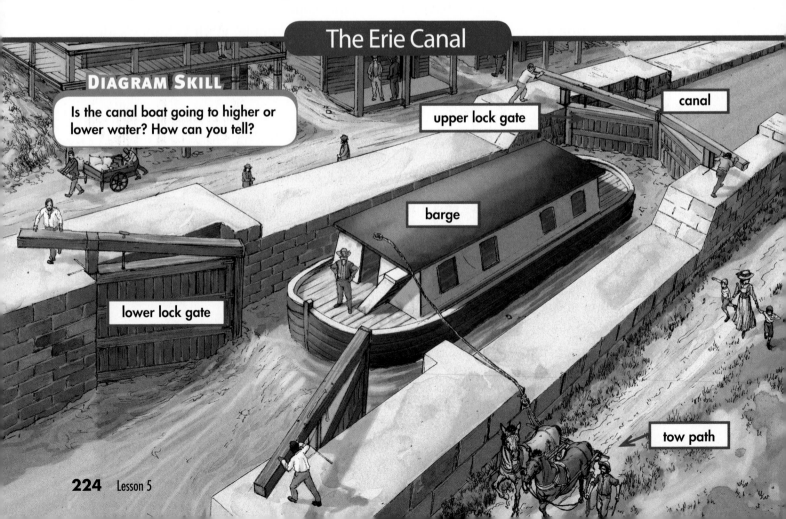

The Erie Canal

DIAGRAM SKILL

Is the canal boat going to higher or lower water? How can you tell?

upper lock gate

canal

barge

lower lock gate

tow path

◀ *Tom Thumb* racing a
horse-drawn carriage

The Iron Horse

People had traveled by railroad for years, but on early railroads, horses pulled coaches over iron rails. In 1814 British inventor George Stephenson built the first train powered by a steam engine. The new trains were nicknamed "iron horses."

In 1830 Peter Cooper, an American merchant, built a small locomotive that he named *Tom Thumb*. At first, few people believed the locomotive could move without horses. A Baltimore stagecoach company challenged Cooper and his locomotive to a race against a horse-drawn carriage. The train lost that race, but trains won in the end. Railroads soon became the main form of transportation in the United States.

QUICK CHECK

Drawing Conclusions How did the invention of the steam engine improve transportation?

Check Understanding

1. **VOCABULARY** Write a short story about the growth of industry in the early 1800s. Use at least two of these terms.

   cotton gin   steam engine

   interchangeable part   reaper

2. **READING SKILL** Draw Conclusions **Use your chart from page 222 to write about the Industrial Revolution.**

Text Clues	Conclusion

3. **Write About It** Write a paragraph explaining how the Erie Canal helped New York City.

THE AGE OF ANDREW JACKSON

Lesson 6

VOCABULARY

Union p. 227

Trail of Tears p. 229

manifest destiny p. 229

wagon train p. 229

discrimination p. 231

READING SKILL

Draw Conclusions
Copy the chart below. As you read, use it to draw a conclusion about the Indian Removal Act.

Text Clues	Conclusion

STANDARDS FOCUS

SOCIAL STUDIES Power, Authority, and Governance.

GEOGRAPHY Places and Regions

Andrew Jackson greets well-wishers before his inauguration in 1829.

Visual Preview

How did freedom change for people?

A President Jackson promised to protect the rights of average Americans.

B Native Americans were forced from their lands as settlers expanded west.

C Immigration from Europe and Asia increased, which helped cities to grow.

A A MAN OF THE PEOPLE

In 1824 new U.S. laws allowed all white men 21 or older—not just wealthy landowners—to vote. This wave of new voters helped elect a new President, a "common man" who would become one of the most controversial Presidents in history.

Andrew Jackson was born in a frontier settlement in the Carolinas. Because of his background, many settlers saw Jackson as someone who shared their values.

Jackson as President

Jackson promised to protect the rights of the Americans who elected him—farmers, frontier settlers, and working people. Under Jackson's leadership, the office of President grew more powerful than it had ever been. Jackson's opponents protested that he was trying to take powers away from Congress.

Trouble in South Carolina

States also protested Jackson's actions. South Carolina lawmakers threatened to leave the **Union** if their state was forced to collect a new federal tax on imported goods. "Union" is the term used for states joined together as one group.

Jackson sent troops and warships to South Carolina to force the state to collect the tax. The crisis passed when the tax was collected. People then accused Jackson of acting more like a king than a President.

QUICK CHECK

Draw Conclusions Why was Jackson popular with settlers but unpopular with state lawmakers?

This political cartoon shows Andrew Jackson as a powerful king who tramples on the Constitution. ▶

Throughout the 1800s, thousands of people moved west. Many people went west to start new lives, find open land, or become wealthy. Others were driven out of their homes and forced to move far away.

Conflict with Native Americans

In the early 1800s, many Native Americans in the Southeast lived peacefully with their white neighbors. Their right to their homeland had been guaranteed by treaties signed with the United States government.

Jackson and some of his supporters believed that Native Americans should leave their lands and allow settlers to live there. Congress passed the Indian Removal Act in 1831. This act forced Native Americans to move to what Congress called the Indian Territory, which is now the state of Oklahoma.

Primary Sources

[In] May 1838 . . . I saw helpless Cherokee arrested and dragged from their homes . . . I saw them loaded like cattle or sheep into six hundred and forty-five wagons and starting toward the west . . . many of the children rose to their feet and waved their little hands good-by to their mountain homes, knowing they were leaving them forever.

A section from *Story of the Trail of Tears* by John G. Burnett, published in 1890

Write About It Write a journal entry in which you describe your thoughts about the removal of Native Americans.

▼ In the Cherokee language, the Trail of Tears is called *Nunna daul Isunyi*—"the Trail Where We Cried." About 4,000 people died along the way. Some who refused to leave their homes were forced into slavery.

Native Americans protested in court. Jackson refused to follow a court ruling allowing Native Americans to remain on their homelands.

In 1838 the United States army forced the Cherokee people to march 800 miles west to the Indian Territory. This journey became known as the **Trail of Tears**. The primary source on page 228 describes what one soldier saw on the Trail of Tears.

Oregon Fever

In the 1840s, Americans became inspired by the idea of **manifest destiny**. This was a belief that the United States had a right to expand its borders and claim new lands. Families began catching "Oregon Fever"—the desire to get a fresh start in the West.

The 2,000-mile journey took six months. Most settlers joined **wagon trains**, a large group of wagons pulled by oxen. Wagon trains offered protection against attacks by Native Americans. People helped one another when wagons broke down. They worked together to cross rivers and make their way through steep mountain passes. Sometimes, Native Americans helped the wagon trains cross difficult regions.

Mormons Settle Utah

Some people were forced to move west because of their religious beliefs. The Church of Jesus Christ of Latter-Day Saints, or the Mormon Church, was founded in New York. The Mormons were forced west in the 1840s. In 1847 the first Mormons arrived at the Great Salt Lake and settled what is now Salt Lake City, Utah.

QUICK CHECK

Draw Conclusions **Why did people travel west together in wagon trains?**

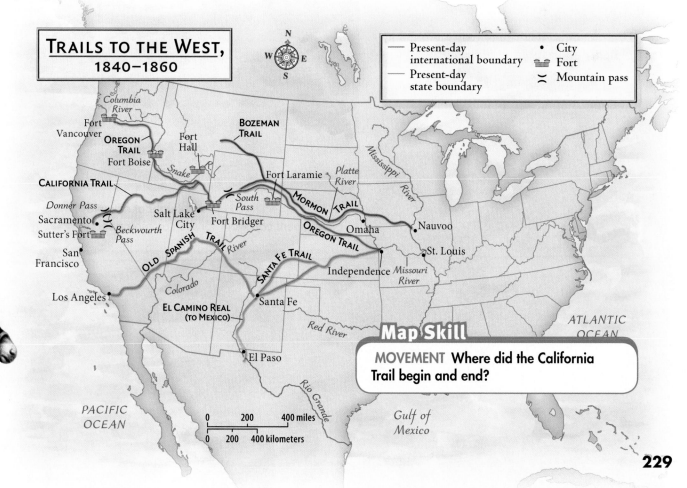

TRAILS TO THE WEST, 1840–1860

- Present-day international boundary
- Present-day state boundary
- • City
- Fort
- ⫯ Mountain pass

Columbia River
Fort Vancouver
OREGON TRAIL
Fort Hall
BOZEMAN TRAIL
Fort Boise
Snake
CALIFORNIA TRAIL
Fort Laramie
Platte River
Mississippi River
Donner Pass
Sacramento
Salt Lake City
South Pass
MORMON TRAIL
Fort Bridger
Beckwourth Pass
Sutter's Fort
OREGON TRAIL
Omaha
Nauvoo
San Francisco
OLD SPANISH TRAIL
River
SANTA FE TRAIL
St. Louis
Los Angeles
Colorado
Independence
Missouri River
EL CAMINO REAL (TO MEXICO)
Santa Fe
Red River
ATLANTIC OCEAN
El Paso
PACIFIC OCEAN
0   200   400 miles
0   200   400 kilometers
Rio Grande
Gulf of Mexico

Map Skill

MOVEMENT **Where did the California Trail begin and end?**

229

Between 1845 and 1860, more immigrants came to the United States than ever before. Many people from Europe and Asia came to find work or to seek fortunes. The Irish left Ireland, their homeland, for a different reason.

The Great Hunger

Starting in 1846, potatoes—Ireland's main food crop for the common people—began to rot because of a plant disease. Irish farmers grew other crops, but the British government forced farmers to send that food to Great Britain. As a result, about 2.5 million people starved to death. The Irish people called this time "The Great Hunger." Between 1846 and 1861, more than one million Irish immigrants came to the United States.

Citizenship
Working for the Common Good

When the United States created the public school system, it was working for the common good. American public schools took on the job of integrating non-English speaking immigrants into American life. Immigrant children were taught civic responsibility, respect for the flag, and even the proper use of the toothbrush.

Write About It Write about new ways the government can work for the common good.

Irish immigrants arriving in New York City in 1847

Free African Americans

By 1850 more than 430,000 free African Americans lived in the United States, mainly in cities where they had found work. Although slavery was illegal in most Northern states, free African Americans still faced **discrimination**. Discrimination is the unfair treatment of people, often based on their race. African Americans did not have equal legal or voting rights to whites. There were places they were not allowed to go.

Cities Grow

In 1820 about 700,000 people lived in all of the cities in the United States. By today's standards, the cities were small.

Port cities like New York grew after the Industrial Revolution because of increased trade. Other active port cities included Boston, Baltimore, Charleston, and New Orleans, which all became major cities.

Almost all immigrants entered the nation through these ports. Some immigrants moved west, but many remained in the cities. By 1840 the population of the nation's cities had risen to about 1.8 million people.

America was growing rapidly within its borders. Meanwhile, in Texas, events were about to change those borders as well.

QUICK CHECK

Draw Conclusions **Why were millions of people forced to leave Ireland between 1846 and 1861?**

Check Understanding

1. **VOCABULARY** Write a sentence for each vocabulary term.

   manifest destiny   discrimination
   wagon train

2. **READING SKILL** Draw Conclusions Use your chart from page 226 to help you write an essay describing the Indian Removal Act.

Text Clues	Conclusion

3. **Write About It** Write about the reasons for the growth of American cities in the 1800s.

Texas and the War with Mexico

Lesson 7

VOCABULARY

Treaty of Guadalupe Hidalgo p. 235

Gold Rush p. 236

READING SKILL

Draw Conclusions

Copy the chart below. As you read, use it to draw a conclusion about the War with Mexico.

Text Clues	Conclusion

STANDARDS FOCUS

SOCIAL STUDIES — Power, Authority, and Governance

GEOGRAPHY — Places and Regions

Mexican soldiers under Santa Anna defeated Texans at the Battle of the Alamo.

Visual Preview

How did conflicts with Mexico change the United States?

A Americans who settled Texas won independence from Mexico in 1836.

B In 1848 the United States won a huge area of land in the War with Mexico.

C The discovery of gold brought thousands of people to California at war's end.

TROUBLE IN TEXAS

In 1821 Mexico won independence from Spain.
At that time, Mexico's northern areas included present-day
Texas, New Mexico, and California.

During those years, few people lived in this huge area. To keep the area under Mexican control, Mexico's government offered land and Mexican citizenship to Americans who settled in Texas.

Americans Settle in Texas

Moses Austin and his son Stephen received almost 18,000 acres in what is present-day Texas. They sold this land to other settlers, bringing in about 300 families. By 1835 about 25,000 Americans lived in this area. Many of these Americans did not want to live in Mexico. They complained about Mexican laws. They also wanted slavery, which was illegal in Mexico, to be legal.

In December 1835 a force of 500 Texans attacked the town of San Antonio. Within days, they took control of the Alamo, a Spanish mission that had been made into a fort.

On March 6, 1836, General Antonio López de Santa Anna, the leader of Mexico, recaptured the Alamo after an almost two-week battle. All of the Americans were killed, but the Texans fought back again. A month later, General Sam Houston surprised a larger Mexican force at San Jacinto near present-day

Houston. The Texans charged, yelling, "Remember the Alamo!" The Texans defeated Santa Ana in less than 20 minutes.

QUICK CHECK

Draw Conclusions **How did a plan to offer land in Texas to American settlers hurt Mexico?**

▲ Stephen Austin

▲ Antonio López de Santa Anna

THE WAR WITH MEXICO

After the victory at the Battle of San Jacinto, Texans voted to join the United States. They adopted a constitution and made slavery legal. The U.S. Congress felt that allowing Texas to join the Union might lead to war with Mexico. Instead, Texas became an independent country—the Republic of Texas. It was also known as the Lone Star Republic.

Beginning the War

In 1845 President James Polk offered to buy the Mexican territories of California and New Mexico for $30 million. When Mexico refused, Polk ordered General Zachary Taylor to march through Texas to the Rio Grande. Fighting broke out with Mexican soldiers there in April 1846. President Polk asked the

James K. Polk ▶

American soldiers invaded Churubusco, Mexico, in 1847.

U.S. Congress for a declaration of war against Mexico, and Congress agreed.

The War Ends

Fighting continued until 1847, when U.S. troops captured Mexico City. The Mexican government signed the **Treaty of Guadalupe Hidalgo** in February 1848. Under this treaty, Mexico sold Texas to the United States for $15 million. The treaty also included land that would become the states of California, Nevada, and Utah as well as parts of Arizona, New Mexico, Colorado, and Wyoming. About 13,000 Americans died during the war, mainly from disease. Thousands more Mexicans died defending their homeland.

QUICK CHECK

Draw Conclusions **How did the War with Mexico help the United States grow?**

Land Acquired from Mexico, 1845–1853

WYOMING
NEVADA
UTAH
COLORADO
KANSAS
CALIFORNIA
Colorado River
Arkansas River
ARIZONA
NEW MEXICO
PACIFIC OCEAN
TEXAS
Rio Grande
MEXICO

- Annexed in 1845
- Mexican land awarded to the U.S. under the Treaty of Guadalupe Hidalgo, 1848
- Gadsden Purchase, 1853
- Present-day boundary

0   150   300 miles
0   150   300 kilometers

N
W   E
S

Map Skill

LOCATION **Which states' borders were expanded in 1853?**

Thousands of "forty-niners" like this man went to California to find gold. Very few struck it rich.

Gold miner

Gold nuggets and pan

C THE CALIFORNIA GOLD RUSH

In January 1848, James Marshall saw something glittering in the American River outside the town of Sacramento, California. It was gold. Marshall tried to keep the discovery a secret, but the news spread. Over the next year, thousands of miners came to search for gold in the area. Prospecting, or exploring for gold, required only a few tools and the willingness to work hard. It was difficult work, and few people struck it rich.

"Gold Fever"

The idea of sudden wealth drew thousands of people to California. So many people came that the event became known as the **Gold Rush**. By May 1849, more than 10,000 wagons had crossed the continent to reach California. In that year alone, more than 80,000 people arrived in California from around the world. Because these people came to California in 1849, they became known as "forty-niners."

▲ Miners often searched for gold in rivers using pans
to separate the gold from pebbles and sand.

The Thirty-First State

By 1850 there were enough people in
California to apply for statehood. Settlers
wanted courts, land and water laws, mail
delivery, and other government services.
On September 9, 1850, President Millard
Fillmore signed a law that made California
the thirty-first state to enter the Union.

QUICK CHECK

Draw Conclusions **Why did the growth of California's
population create a desire for statehood?**

Check Understanding

1. VOCABULARY Write a paragraph using the
vocabulary terms to explain how California
became a state.

Treaty of Guadalupe Hidalgo

Gold Rush

2. READING SKILL Draw
Conclusions Use your chart from
page 232 to help you write about
the War with Mexico.

Text Clues	Conclusion

3. Write About It Write about
how the desire to grow wealthy caused
a huge increase in California's
population.

237

Vocabulary

Number a paper from 1 to 4. Beside each number, write the word below that matches the description.

bill of rights   **Trail of Tears**

pioneers   **manifest destiny**

1. The belief that the United States was meant to expand its borders

2. A formal statement of rights and liberties guaranteed to the people by a state

3. The people who are the first to enter a new land or region

4. The forced march of Native Americans to Indian Territory

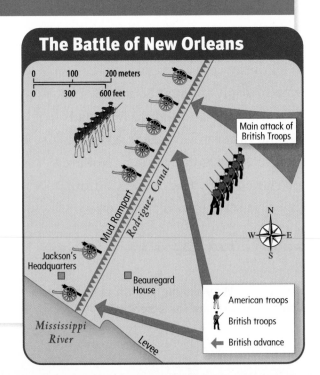

Comprehension and Critical Thinking

5. Why did the U.S. Congress pass the Embargo Act?

6. **Reading Skill** Why did U.S. farmers, settlers, and working-class people support Andrew Jackson?

7. **Critical Thinking** How did the Great Compromise affect the way states were represented?

8. **Critical Thinking** What effect did the Industrial Revolution have on farming?

Skill

Compare Maps at Different Scales

Write a complete sentence to answer each question.

9. What is the difference between a large-scale and a small-scale map?

10. Compare the map on the right with the map on page 219. Which map is an example of a small-scale map? How do you know?

The Battle of New Orleans

0   100   200 meters
0   300   600 feet

Main attack of British Troops

Mud Rampart

Rodriguez Canal

Jackson's Headquarters

Beauregard House

N
W E
S

American troops

British troops

British advance

Mississippi River

Levee

Test Preparation

Use the time line below to answer the questions.

The Industrial Revolution

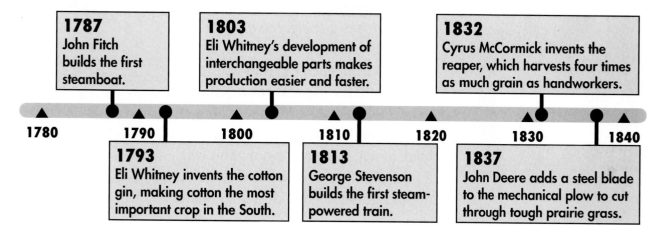

1787 John Fitch builds the first steamboat.

1803 Eli Whitney's development of interchangeable parts makes production easier and faster.

1832 Cyrus McCormick invents the reaper, which harvests four times as much grain as handworkers.

1780   1790   1800   1810   1820   1830   1840

1793 Eli Whitney invents the cotton gin, making cotton the most important crop in the South.

1813 George Stevenson builds the first steam-powered train.

1837 John Deere adds a steel blade to the mechanical plow to cut through tough prairie grass.

1. The spinning machine was invented in 1790. If this invention were added to the time line, where would it be placed?

   A. After the steam-powered train

   B. After the steamboat

   C. After the reaper

   D. After the cotton gin

2. Which invention mentioned on the time line involved transportation?

   A. The plow

   B. The cotton gin

   C. The steamboat

   D. Interchangeable parts

3. Which inventor helped to create conditions for slavery to expand?

   A. Eli Whitney

   B. John Fitch

   C. John Deere

   D. Cyrus McCormick

4. Give four examples of how the Industrial Revolution changed people's lives.

5. Why was the word "Revolution" used to describe this period?

The Big Idea — Activities

What causes a society to grow?

Write About the Big Idea

Expository Essay

Use the Unit 5 Foldable to help you write an expository essay that answers the Big Idea question, "*What causes a society to grow?*" Begin with an introduction. Choose one item from each tab that you think made the biggest contribution to society's growth. Write a paragraph that explains why you have drawn that conclusion. End with a paragraph naming the single most important reason for society's growth.

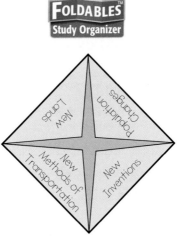

FOLDABLES™
Study Organizer

New Lands

Population Changes

New Methods of Transportation

New Inventions

The Constitution: What's Most Important?

Now that you have read about the Constitution, decide which part of the important document means the most to you. Write a speech as if you are one of these sections of the Constitution:

Preamble

Article I (Legislative Branch)

Article II (Executive Branch)

Article III (Judicial Branch)

Bill of Rights

We the People

Complete these sentences

I am _____ the most important part of the Constitution.

My job is to _____.

Without me, _____.

When you have finished giving your speeches, hold a class election to decide the most important part of the Constitution.

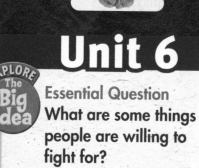

Unit 6

EXPLORE
The **Big Idea**

Essential Question
What are some things people are willing to fight for?

FOLDABLES™
Study Organizer

Fact and Opinion
Make and label a Two-tab Foldable before you read this unit. Across the top, write **Things people fight for.** Label the two tabs **North** and **South.** Use the Foldable to organize information as you read.

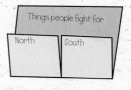

Things people fight for

North   South

LOG ON

Find out more about the Civil War at
www.macmillanmh.com

During the Civil War, many soldiers from the North and the South died on the battlefields.

Slavery AND Emancipation

PEOPLE, PLACES, AND EVENTS

Jermain Loguen

Clara Barton

New York

1859 Jermain Loguen is a station master on the Underground Railroad.

Maryland

1862 Clara Barton cares for wounded Union soldiers at the Battle of Antietam.

1855

1860

By 1859 **Jermain Loguen** had helped more than 1,500 enslaved people escape to freedom.

Today you can see the property in **Syracuse, New York**, where Loguen hid people who escaped slavery.

In 1862 **Clara Barton** helped care for Union soldiers wounded at the **Battle of Antietam.**

Today you can the visit the Antietam National Battlefield in Maryland.

Ulysses S. Grant

Robert E. Lee

Mississippi

1863 | Union soldiers under Grant take Vicksburg, Mississippi.

Virginia

1865 | General Robert E. Lee surrenders at Appomattox Court House.

1865

1870

In July 1863, Union troops under General **Ulysses S. Grant** defeated Confederate forces at **Vicksburg** on the Mississippi River.

Today you can tour the Vicksburg National Military Park in Mississippi.

In 1865 Confederate General **Robert E. Lee** surrendered to Union General Ulysses S. Grant at **Appomattox Court House**, Virginia.

Today you can travel to the McLean House where Lee and Grant met.

KING COTTON AND THE SPREAD OF SLAVERY

Cotton was the most important cash crop in the Southern economy during the 1800s.

VOCABULARY

slave state p. 246

free state p. 246

Missouri Compromise p. 246

tariff p. 247

READING SKILL

Fact and Opinion

Copy the chart below. As you read, fill in facts about the North and South.

Fact	Opinion

STANDARDS FOCUS

SOCIAL STUDIES People, Places, and Environments

GEOGRAPHY Environment and Society

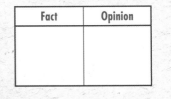

Visual Preview

How did the South affect the nation's economy and politics?

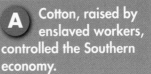

A Cotton, raised by enslaved workers, controlled the Southern economy.

B The issues of slavery and the economy divided the North and South.

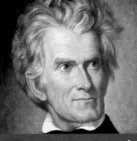

C Congress passed taxes on imported goods, which angered Southern leaders.

244

A COTTON RULES THE SOUTH

The hot climate and moist soil of the South were perfect for growing cotton. In the 1800s it became the most important cash crop in the South. By the 1830s Southerners called their crop "King Cotton."

Plantation owners used enslaved Africans to work in cotton fields. Many owners grew wealthy from selling cotton harvested by enslaved workers. It was sold mainly to Great Britain, where factories made the cotton into cloth.

Cotton plants weakened the soil. Planters needed more land, so they moved west. Cotton fields spread across Tennessee, Alabama, Mississippi, and, eventually, across the Mississippi River to Arkansas and Texas.

▲ The cotton gin removed the seeds from cotton bolls.

Enslaved Population Grows

The growth of cotton as a cash crop and the movement to the west created a need for more enslaved workers. In 1806 Congress passed a law that said no enslaved people could be brought into the United States after 1808. This law did not bring an end to slavery. The population of enslaved people continued to grow because the children of enslaved people were also enslaved. In addition, planters often brought enslaved people into the country from Caribbean islands.

Southern Economy

The economy of the South was built on the labor of enslaved workers. The wealthiest Southerners owned large areas of land and had thousands of enslaved workers. Most Southern farmers planted crops on small pieces of land. They did not have enslaved workers. Even so, both plantation owners and small farmers depended on cotton.

Farmers grew food for the plantations, repaired roads, and built wagons. When the cotton was harvested, some farmers earned money transporting crops to Southern ports by wagon.

QUICK CHECK

Fact and Opinion **What is a fact about cotton?**

In 1819 Missouri applied to be admitted to the Union as a **slave state**, a state in which slavery is allowed. At the time, the nation had 11 slave states and 11 **free states**, or states in which slavery was not allowed. Allowing Missouri to enter the Union as a slave state would upset the balance in Congress. Slave states would have more votes in the Senate than free states. Northern states wanted to keep the political balance in Congress.

Both sides argued over Missouri for a year. Finally, Senator Henry Clay of Kentucky solved the problem with the **Missouri Compromise**. Under this plan, Missouri was admitted as a slave state. Maine, which had been part of Massachusetts, came in as a free state. The compromise stated that in the future, slavery would not be allowed in any new states north of Missouri's southern border.

Economic Differences

Slavery was not the only issue that divided the North and South. The regions had important economic differences. Cotton was king in the South. Even people who did not grow cotton worked in some way to help bring it to market.

Unlike the South, the Northern economy was based on industry. These industries did not use enslaved workers. This fact led states in the North to outlaw slavery. In 1777 Vermont became the first state to outlaw slavery. Then, in 1804, New Jersey became the last Northern state to outlaw slavery.

Map Skill

LOCATION **Which states made up a larger area of the United States—slave states or free states?**

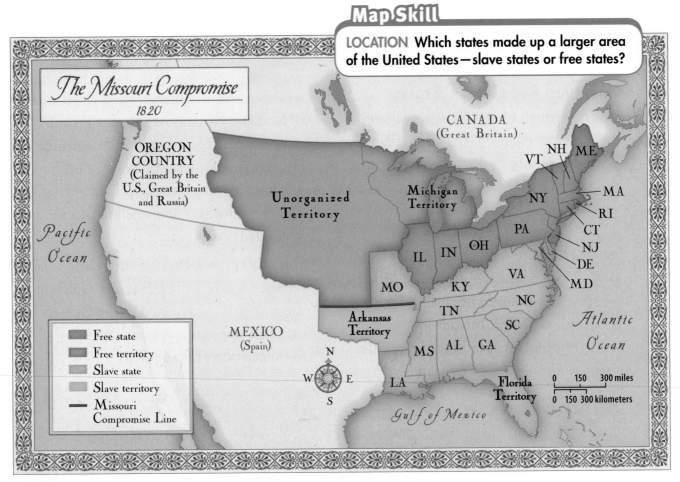

The Missouri Compromise 1820

CANADA (Great Britain)

OREGON COUNTRY (Claimed by the U.S., Great Britain and Russia)

Unorganized Territory

Michigan Territory

Pacific Ocean

MEXICO (Spain)

Arkansas Territory

Florida Territory

Gulf of Mexico

Atlantic Ocean

Legend:
- Free state
- Free territory
- Slave state
- Slave territory
- Missouri Compromise Line

0   150   300 miles
0   150   300 kilometers

▲ Many Northern factories used women and children as workers. Cotton dresses, such as the dress on the left, were made in Northern factories.

In the North, men, women, and even children worked in factories making cloth, iron tools, rope, and other products. These factories were small compared to those of Great Britain. Also, British factories used new technology to make many of the same products more cheaply. That meant they could sell their products to Americans at prices lower than those charged by U.S. manufacturers.

Lower prices made it difficult for Americans who owned small factories to compete with British factories. American businesses that could not sell their more costly products failed. As a result, business owners asked Congress to pass **tariffs**, or special taxes on goods coming into the United States. Tariffs raised the price of foreign-made products and helped American industries. In 1828 Congress passed tariffs on British goods, which pleased Northern business owners.

QUICK CHECK

Fact and Opinion Why would a Northern factory owner want tariffs on British goods?

The new tariffs angered people in the South. Small farmers complained that tariffs raised the price of imports, or goods brought into the country. In fact, imported goods often cost more anyway. The tariffs also angered plantation owners. High tariffs meant that British manufacturers sold fewer goods in the United States. Fewer sales meant Great Britain had less money to buy cotton. This hurt Southern exports, or goods shipped out of the country.

▲ Senator John C. Calhoun of South Carolina spoke out against tariffs.

Speaking Out Against Congress

Southerners believed the tariffs threatened their way of life. Senator John C. Calhoun of South Carolina spoke out against the tariffs. He claimed Congress was trying to destroy the Southern economy. He said Congress was using tariffs to force the South to end the use of enslaved workers.

Calhoun said the Constitution gave states the right to ignore the laws passed by Congress if those laws hurt the state. Many Americans, including President Andrew Jackson, strongly disagreed with Calhoun. They thought that allowing states to decide which federal laws to obey could destroy the Union.

Jackson sent U.S. forces to South Carolina to enforce the tariffs. This use of federal troops caused even greater anger in the South. It would eventually be one cause of the bloodiest war in United States history.

QUICK CHECK

Fact and Opinion **Why did John C. Calhoun speak out against tariffs?**

Check Understanding

1. **VOCABULARY** Write a sentence using the word that is not related to the other three.

   slave state   Missouri Compromise
   free state   tariff

2. **READING SKILL Fact and Opinion.** Use the chart from page 244 to write your opinions about the facts you have listed.

North	
South	

3. **Write About It** Why did Southerners fight to bring slavery into Missouri?

Chart and Graph Skills
Climographs

VOCABULARY

climate
climograph

You have read that the climate in the South was perfect for growing cotton. One way to learn more about **climate**, or the weather of a place over a number of years, is to study a **climograph**. A climograph shows the temperature, precipitation, and other climate information of a place over time. The climograph below shows the climate of Memphis, Tennessee.

Learn It

- Study the labels on the climograph. Notice that it is really two graphs in one: a bar graph and a line graph.

- Study the scales of measurement on the climograph. Precipitation is shown in the blue bar graph that measures inches, shown on the left. Temperature is shown by a line graph that measures the average temperature in degrees Fahrenheit, shown on the right.

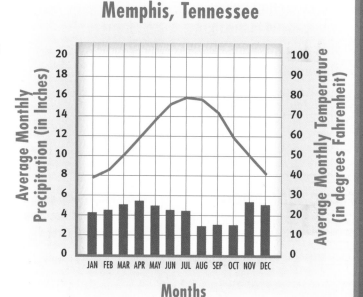

Memphis, Tennessee

Try It

- What is Memphis's average temperature in July?

- Which months have the greatest amount of precipitation? Which have the least?

Apply It

- Research the climate of a place you would like to visit.

- What are some ways you could use a climograph?

Heading Toward War

VOCABULARY

abolitionists p. 251

debate p. 255

treason p. 256

secede p. 257

civil war p. 257

READING SKILL

Fact and Opinion
Copy the chart below. As you read, fill in the right side with opinions about slavery and abolition.

Fact	Opinion

STANDARDS FOCUS

SOCIAL STUDIES   Power, Authority, and Governance

GEOGRAPHY   The Uses of Geography

Many people who escaped slavery headed North on the Underground Railroad.

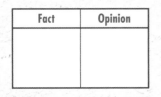

Visual Preview

How did the issue of slavery affect the United States?

A Abolitionists from the North and South helped enslaved people in different ways.

B New laws increased conflict over slavery in the North and South.

C Political events, such as the Dred Scott decision, further divided Americans.

D After Lincoln was elected President, the South left the Union.

A THE FIGHT OVER SLAVERY

Between 1820 and 1860, no issue divided the United States more than slavery. Some people said slavery was morally wrong. Others claimed it was necessary to preserve their way of life.

By the 1830s, many Americans wanted to abolish, or end, slavery. These people were called **abolitionists**.

Among the abolitionists were two sisters who grew up in South Carolina—Angelina and Sarah Grimké. Angelina said the abolition of slavery was:

"a cause worth dying for."

Immediate Release

One abolitionist leader was William Lloyd Garrison of Massachusetts. In 1831 he founded *The Liberator*, an abolitionist newspaper. In 1833 Garrison founded the American Anti-Slavery Society.

Another well-known person who spoke out against slavery was Frederick Douglass. He was born into slavery. After escaping, Douglass gave speeches about his early life. He also published an antislavery newspaper, *The North Star*.

In 1852 Harriet Beecher Stowe wrote *Uncle Tom's Cabin.* Her novel described a cruel slaveholder's treatment of enslaved people. This book turned many people against slavery.

Frederick Douglass

The Underground Railroad

In the 1830s, enslaved people, free African Americans, and white abolitionists started the Underground Railroad, a secret network of trails, river crossings, and hiding places.

Many railroad terms had double meanings on this network. Enslaved people who decided to escape were called *passengers. Conductors* helped enslaved people escape. The houses where enslaved people could eat and rest were called *stations.*

Jermain Loguen was one of the many sucessful conductors on the Underground Railroad. He had escaped from slavery and wanted to help other people gain their freedom. His home in Syracuse, New York, became a well-known station. Harriet Tubman, an escaped enslaved woman, was a famous conductor who led many enslaved people North to freedom.

QUICK CHECK

Fact and Opinion **Was Angelina Grimké's statement a fact or an opinion?**

COMPROMISE LEADS TO VIOLENCE

Congress tried to settle the slavery issue with compromises. As new territories applied to enter the Union, however, slavery continued to divide lawmakers and the American people.

Compromise of 1850

The U.S. victory in the War with Mexico of 1846–1848 brought large areas of land under U.S. control. In 1849 California applied to join the Union as a free state. This would change the balance of 15 free and 15 slave states. As in 1820, neither side wanted the other to gain control in the Senate. Southern lawmakers refused to admit California. In the end, Congress agreed to the Compromise of 1850. This allowed California to enter the Union. In return, Congress passed the Fugitive Slave Law. This law forced Americans to return runaway enslaved people to the person who had held them, or go to jail. Many Northerners were angered by the law.

The Southern attack on Lawrence, Kansas, was the first battle of what newspapers called "Bleeding Kansas." ▼

John Brown

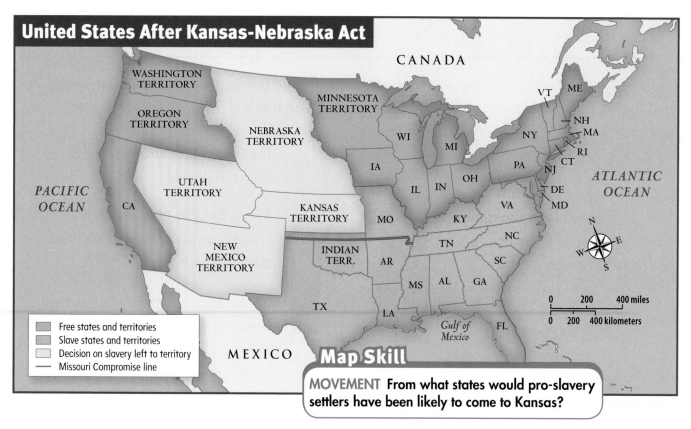

United States After Kansas-Nebraska Act

CANADA

WASHINGTON TERRITORY

OREGON TERRITORY

MINNESOTA TERRITORY

NEBRASKA TERRITORY

VT
ME
NH
MA
RI
CT
NJ
DE
MD

WI
MI
NY
PA

IA
OH
IL
IN

PACIFIC OCEAN

CA

UTAH TERRITORY

KANSAS TERRITORY

MO
KY
VA

ATLANTIC OCEAN

NEW MEXICO TERRITORY

INDIAN TERR.

AR

TN
NC
SC

MS
AL
GA

TX

LA

FL

Gulf of Mexico

MEXICO

N
W E
S

0   200   400 miles
0   200   400 kilometers

Free states and territories
Slave states and territories
Decision on slavery left to territory
Missouri Compromise line

Map Skill

MOVEMENT From what states would pro-slavery settlers have been likely to come to Kansas?

Kansas-Nebraska Act

In 1854 Congress created two new territories, Kansas and Nebraska. Under the Missouri Compromise, neither territory could allow slavery. This changed when Senator Stephen Douglas of Illinois introduced the Kansas-Nebraska Act. In this act, Douglas used the term *popular sovereignty.* This meant that people—not the federal government—would vote to accept or ban slavery. This act overturned the Missouri Compromise.

New Political Party

The passage of the Kansas-Nebraska Act led Northern abolitionists to form a new political party, the Republicans. A lawyer from Illinois named Abraham Lincoln joined the Republican Party. Lincoln believed slavery was wrong, but he did not call for it to be abolished immediately. Lincoln wanted to stop slavery from spreading to new states.

"Bleeding Kansas"

After the passage of the Kansas-Nebraska Act, many Southerners moved to Kansas. They came to vote under popular sovereignty. Northern abolitionists responded by moving to Kansas. Suddenly armed settlers supporting both sides of the issue flooded the area.

Violence finally broke out in 1856, when settlers who favored slavery burned the free town of Lawrence, Kansas, to the ground. A few days later, abolitionist John Brown and his sons killed five Southerners. Newspapers began to describe the territory as "Bleeding Kansas." The violence in Kansas did not become all-out war, but it was a preview of events to come.

QUICK CHECK

Fact and Opinion What opinion would abolitionists have had about the Fugitive Slave Law?

253

C   A NATION DIVIDED

By 1857, the United States was close to breaking apart. Many Americans wondered whether the country could survive half-free and half-slave.

A Case About Freedom

In 1857 a case about the rights of enslaved people came before the United States Supreme Court. It was the case of *Dred Scott* v. *Sanford*. Dred Scott was an enslaved person bought by a doctor in Missouri, a slave state. The doctor moved his household to Illinois, a free state, and then to the Wisconsin Territory, where slavery was banned by the Northwest Ordinance of 1787.

Years later, the doctor and his household returned to Missouri. When the doctor died,

▲ Dred Scott

Scott said he was a free man because he had lived on free soil. Eleven years later, the Supreme Court refused to free Scott. Chief Justice Roger Taney wrote that enslaved people could be:

❝ . . . bought and sold and treated as an ordinary article of merchandise. ❞

The court's decision meant that enslaved workers could be taken anywhere, even free states, and remain enslaved.

In 1857, most Northerners didn't want to abolish slavery in the South. They didn't want slavery in new territories. This issue would soon become important in a political campaign.

Lincoln Against Douglas

In 1858 two candidates from Illinois attracted national attention. Abraham Lincoln, a Republican, ran against Stephen Douglas, a Democrat, for the Senate. Compared to the popular Douglas, Lincoln was unknown.

The two candidates held seven **debates**, or public discussions, on political issues. The three-hour debates drew crowds as large as 15,000. The candidates argued over many issues, but the issue of slavery drew the most attention.

Although Douglas disliked slavery, he refused to speak out against it. He believed popular sovereignty was the way to resolve disagreement over slavery. Douglas tried to paint Lincoln as a reckless abolitionist.

Lincoln believed that slavery was wrong for a nation founded on freedom. In a speech during the campaign, Lincoln said,

"This government cannot endure permanently half-slave and half-free."

Lincoln received more votes than Douglas in the election. At that time, state legislatures chose Senators for the state. The Democrats held more seats in the Illinois legislature, and they picked Douglas, a Democrat. In the end, the campaign helped Lincoln. Republicans from the North and the Midwest agreed that he would be a good presidential candidate.

QUICK CHECK

Fact and Opinion Write one fact and one opinion about the Lincoln-Douglas campaign.

▼ The Lincoln-Douglas debates drew large crowds. Newspapers across the country reported on the debates.

By 1859 many Americans feared that war would soon tear apart the nation. There seemed to be no way to avoid violence.

John Brown's Raid

For John Brown, there was no compromise on slavery. The fierce abolitionist had been a conductor on the Underground Railroad in New York. He was also involved in the violent events in "Bleeding Kansas." In 1859 Brown tried to start a revolt among enslaved people. He planned to attack an Army arsenal in Harpers Ferry, Virginia. Brown then planned to give the weapons to enslaved people who he believed would rise up against plantation owners. On October 16, Brown and a small force captured the arsenal. Enslaved people nearby did not join him, or revolt against the slaveholders. Two days later, U.S. soldiers, commanded by Colonel Robert E. Lee, recaptured the arsenal. Brown was convicted of **treason**, or betraying one's country, and hanged. His raid struck fear across the South.

The Election of 1860

In the presidential election of 1860, Abraham Lincoln ran as the Republican candidate. Stephen Douglas ran as a Democrat.

▼ The Civil War began with an attack by Confederate artillery on Fort Sumter in Charleston, South Carolina, on April 12, 1861.

Two other candidates also joined the race. Only Lincoln took a stand against slavery in the new territories. Southern lawmakers warned that if Lincoln won, they would **secede**, or withdraw, from the Union.

In November 1860, Lincoln was elected. Then, in December, South Carolina was the first state to secede. By February, six more states had seceded. They established the Confederate States of America, also called the Confederacy, and elected Jefferson Davis as their President.

▲ Abraham Lincoln

First Shots Fired

In the spring of 1861, Confederate troops seized several U. S. Army arsenals in the South. Fort Sumter, an island arsenal in the harbor of Charleston, South Carolina, refused to surrender. The commander asked the federal government for more supplies and weapons. Before supplies could arrive, Confederate guns fired on the fort on April 12, 1861. The Civil War had begun. A **civil war** is a war among people who live in the same country.

QUICK CHECK

Fact and Opinion What event between 1859 and 1861 was most responsible for causing the Civil War?

Check Understanding

1. **VOCABULARY** Write a summary of this lesson using the vocabulary terms.

   abolitionist   secede
   debate   civil war

2. **READING SKILL Fact and Opinion** Use the chart from page 250 to write your personal opinion about John Brown.

Fact	Opinion

3. **Write About It** Why were the settlers in Kansas ready to use violence?

VOCABULARY

draft p. 259

Anaconda Plan p. 262

total war p. 264

READING SKILL

Fact and Opinion

Copy the chart below. As you read, record the opinions of each side.

Fact	Opinion

STANDARDS FOCUS

SOCIAL STUDIES — Power, Authority, and Governance

GEOGRAPHY — The Uses of Geography

The Nation Divided by War

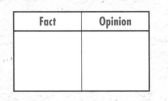

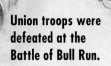

Union troops were defeated at the Battle of Bull Run.

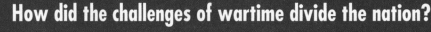

Visual Preview

How did the challenges of wartime divide the nation?

A The South won the first major battle of the war at Bull Run.

B Both the North and South had specific strengths and weaknesses.

C Early battles proved the war would be long and bloody.

D The Civil War was a total war, one in which each side also strikes against civilians.

A THE WAR BEGINS

In the beginning, leaders in both the North and South thought the Civil War would last about two months. Some soldiers even feared the war would be over before they had a chance to fight.

By 1862 people on both sides realized the war was turning into a long, drawn-out conflict. The Civil War would become the bloodiest war in American history.

Battle of Bull Run

The first major battle of the Civil War was fought on July 21, 1861. It took place at a stream called Bull Run, near the town of Manassas, Virginia. Manassas is located between Washington, D.C., and Richmond, Virginia. Richmond was the capital of the Confederacy. That day, sightseers followed the Union troops. Many expected to watch a rapid Union victory. Then Richmond would fall quickly. What they saw instead was bloodshed and death.

For hours, Union soldiers attacked the line of Confederate soldiers, but could not break through. General Thomas Jackson was standing firm with his troops. One Confederate officer shouted:

"There stands Jackson like a stone wall!"

From that day forward, "Stonewall" Jackson became a Confederate hero.

With the battlefield littered with bloody bodies, fresh Southern troops arrived by railroad. Soon, Northern troops retreated in panic. Frightened soldiers and panicked sightseers fled to Washington. The South had won the first major battle of the war.

At first, excitement about the war made many Northern and Southern men eager to join the fight. As the war dragged on, the death toll rose. Both sides had to use a **draft**. A draft is the selection of men who must serve in the military. Draft riots broke out in many Northern cities.

QUICK CHECK

Fact and Opinion What opinion did leaders on both sides share at the beginning of the war?

PLACES

The Battle of Bull Run was fought at **Manassas, Virginia.** Today Manassas is a suburb of Washington, D.C. You can visit the museum at Manassas National Battlefield Park, where the battle was fought.

Manassas, Virginia

B STRENGTHS AND WEAKNESSES

Many Southerners believed they would win the war because they had a stronger military tradition than the North. Its generals had more experience. Confederate soldiers grew up riding horses and hunting. Large numbers of Southerners volunteered to fight. They were eager to protect their homes and way of life.

THE CONFEDERACY

STRENGTHS

- It planned a defensive war, which is easier for the military to win.

- A third of the nation's officers joined the Confederate army, including Robert E. Lee, the most respected general in the Army.

- It had a strong military tradition, with 7 of the nation's 8 military schools located in the South.

- Southerners were more skilled in shooting, hunting, and riding.

- Soldiers began preparing for war before the attack on Fort Sumter.

WEAKNESSES

- It had less than half the population of the North, and one-third were enslaved people.

- The South had less money to support the war effort than did the North.

- The South had only one factory producing cannons and no major factory for making gunpowder.

- The South had half as many miles of railroad track as the North, making it difficult to get food, weapons, and other supplies to troops.

Northerners were also brave fighters. But many lived in cities, so the military tradition was not as strong as it was in the South. Even so, Northerners believed they would win simply because they had more people, industry, and money than the South.

QUICK CHECK

Fact and Opinion What did Southerners think about their military tradition?

THE UNION

STRENGTHS	WEAKNESSES
• In 1861 the North had more than twice the population of the South.	• Union troops fought mostly in Southern areas, where people were defending their homes.
• More than three-quarters of U.S. Navy officers came from the North, and 90 percent of the Navy stayed with the North.	• Long supply lines made it difficult for Union troops to move quickly.
• About 80 percent of U.S. factories were in the North.	• Many Northern soldiers came from areas where there was little military tradition.
• The majority of railroads were in the North.	• Most Union soldiers had little military training.
• Almost all firearms were manufactured in the North.	• Union armies would have to take control of most of the South to bring it back into the Union.
• Northern farms grew more food than Southern farms.	

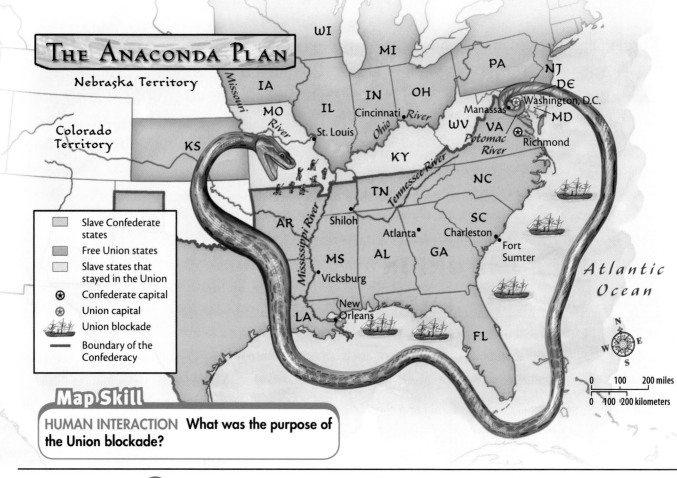

THE ANACONDA PLAN

Nebraska Territory

Colorado Territory

WI

MI

PA

NJ

DE

IA

Washington, D.C.

MN

MO

IL

IN

OH

Cincinnati

Ohio River

Manassas

MD

St. Louis

WV

VA

Richmond

KS

Potomac River

KY

Tennessee River

TN

NC

Missouri River

AR

Shiloh

SC

Atlanta

Charleston

Fort Sumter

Mississippi River

MS

AL

GA

Atlantic Ocean

Vicksburg

New Orleans

LA

FL

Legend:
- Slave Confederate states
- Free Union states
- Slave states that stayed in the Union
- Confederate capital
- Union capital
- Union blockade
- Boundary of the Confederacy

0   100   200 miles
0   100   200 kilometers

N E S W

Map Skill

HUMAN INTERACTION What was the purpose of the Union blockade?

ⓒ THE WAR CONTINUES

General Winfield Scott, the commander of the Union Army, made a plan to win the war. This plan would make it more difficult for the South to get the supplies it needed to fight the war. He called it the **Anaconda Plan**. Look at the map of the Anaconda Plan on this page.

The Anaconda Plan

An anaconda is a giant snake that strangles its prey. That is exactly what General Scott wanted to do to the South. Scott's Anaconda Plan had three parts. First, Northern ships would cut off, or blockade, Southern seaports. Without trade, the South would be unable to buy weapons and supplies. Second, the North would take control of the Mississippi River. This would divide the South and prevent Confederates from using the river to move supplies. In the final part of the plan, Union troops would invade the South, squeezing the region from both the east and the west.

The South's Strategy

While the North worked on its Anaconda Plan, the South prepared to defend its homeland. Jefferson Davis, president of the Confederacy, knew that a Union blockade of Southern ports could destroy the Confederate economy. Davis also knew that Great Britain and France needed Southern cotton. He believed British ships would break the Union blockade. Davis soon realized he was wrong. Europe had a surplus of cotton in the 1860s. Also, the British and French did not want to get involved in a foreign war. Look at the datagraphic on page 263. Which side, the North or the South, had the greater number of resources to fight the war?

The Battle of Shiloh

The number of casualties, or dead and wounded, at Bull Run shocked people on both sides. But those numbers were slight compared to those at the Battle of Shiloh, in Tennessee. There, on April 6, 1862, a Confederate army under General Albert Sidney Johnston surprised a Union army commanded by General Ulysses S. Grant.

It was the first time under fire for most of the soldiers. Still, the South pushed back one Union position after another. At one spot along a sunken road, bullets buzzed through the air. The place became known as "The Hornet's Nest."

The next day, dead bodies covered the bloody battlefield. The Union troops were near defeat. Suddenly, a second Union army arrived. The tired Confederates could not hold off a fresh Union attack. The North won at Shiloh, but both sides paid a heavy price. Twice as many Americans died in this one battle as died in the entire American Revolution. Shiloh showed both sides that the war would be long and bloody. Never again would people go sightseeing at the scene of a battle. What they saw would be too terrible.

QUICK CHECK

Fact and Opinion **How did opinions about the war change after the Battle of Shiloh?**

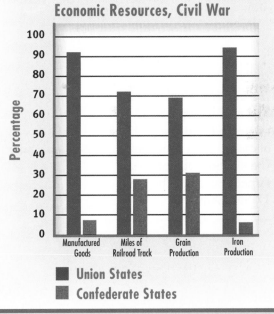

DataGraphic

Resources of the North and the South

Both the North and the South expected to win the Civil War. Study the chart and graph below. Then answer the questions.

Human Resources, Civil War

	Troops	Population
Union States	2,000,000	23,000,000
Confederate States	800,000	9,000,000

Economic Resources, Civil War

Percentage (y-axis: 0 to 100)

Categories (x-axis): Manufactured Goods, Miles of Railroad Track, Grain Production, Iron Production

■ Union States
■ Confederate States

Think About Resources

1. Why did the North have more troops?

2. Why was iron an important resource?

◀ Twice as many Americans were killed at Shiloh as were killed in the American Revolution.

The Civil War was different from earlier American wars because it reached beyond battlefields. Farms and cities were burned. People were terrorized. Some historians call the Civil War the first **total war**. In a total war, each side strikes against the economic system and civilians of the other. Civilians are people who are not in the armed forces. In total war, entire populations are pulled into the conflict.

New Technology

Technology transformed the way the Civil War was fought. Railroads and telegraphs changed the way generals made battlefield decisions. Technology also made the Civil War more deadly than earlier wars. Rifles could fire bullets longer distances with greater accuracy. Mines were used to surprise and kill the enemy. Iron-covered battle ships, called ironclads, made wooden ships seem outdated overnight—cannon balls bounced off the hard metal sides.

The Confederates built the first ironclad ship, the CSS *Virginia*, formerly the USS *Merrimack*. To counter this new threat, the Union built the ironclad, USS *Monitor*. On March 9, 1862, the two ironclads fought off the Virginia coast. Neither ship could sink the other. Still, it was a victory for the North because they kept their blockade in place. Then one month later, the Union captured the port of New Orleans. Continuing the

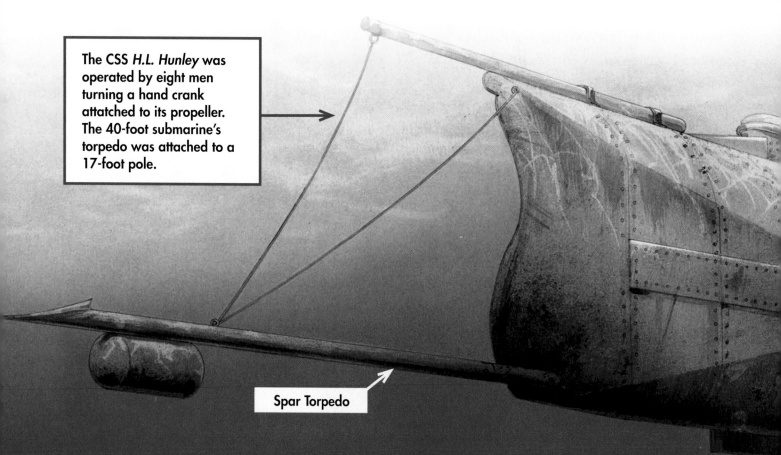

The CSS *H.L. Hunley* was operated by eight men turning a hand crank attached to its propeller. The 40-foot submarine's torpedo was attached to a 17-foot pole.

Spar Torpedo

Anaconda Plan, Union ships began to sail up the Mississippi River. Soon, the Union navy controlled the river.

After the battle of the ironclads, "*Monitor* fever" swept the nation. Ironclad railroad cars were manufactured. With their thick armor plates and cannons, they were similar to modern tanks. Both sides also experimented with mines, torpedoes, and submarines. The South tried many ways to break the Union blockade of its ports. One Confederate, Horace L. Hunley, invented a submarine to sink warships. On February 16, 1864, the CSS *H.L. Hunley* sank the USS *Housatonic* near the Port of Charleston. Soon after the attack, however, the *Hunley* also sank. It may have been damaged during the blast. Even though the mission was a success, the port remained under Union control. The Union's ability to cut off the South's supplies would have a significant effect on the outcome of the Civil War.

QUICK CHECK

Fact and Opinion What is your opinion of total war?

Check Understanding

1. **VOCABULARY** Choose one word and write a paragraph explaining how it was used as a strategy in the Civil War.

   Anaconda Plan   **total war**

2. **READING SKILL Fact and Opinion** Use your chart from page 258 to write your opinion about the most important strength of each side.

Fact	Opinion

3. **Write About It** Write about the reasons soldiers from the South and North fought in the Civil War.

Handcrank

Propeller

The Union Moves Toward Victory

A reenactment of the Battle of Antietam

Lesson 4

VOCABULARY

Emancipation Proclamation p. 267

Gettysburg Address p. 271

READING SKILL

Fact and Opinion

Copy the chart below. As you read, fill in the chart with two facts and two of your own opinions about the Gettysburg Address.

Fact	Opinion

STANDARDS FOCUS

 SOCIAL STUDIES Individual Development and Identity

GEOGRAPHY Human Systems

Visual Preview

How did civil war impact life in the United States?

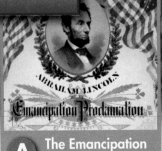

A The Emancipation Proclamation ended slavery in Confederate states.

B Free African Americans enlisted, and the Union won at Vicksburg.

C The Union victory at Gettysburg changed the course of the war for the North.

D Women supported war both at home and on the war front.

Ⓐ BATTLE OF ANTIETAM

For months, Lincoln wanted to make an announcement that would change the purpose of the Civil War. He needed to do it after a Union victory. That victory finally came on September 17, 1862, the bloodiest day in American history.

After winning several battles in Virginia, Robert E. Lee's Confederate army marched north into Maryland in September 1862. Lee planned to continue east and surround Washington, D.C. The Confederates encountered the Union army at Antietam Creek near Sharpsburg, Maryland, on September 17. When the fighting ended that day, nearly 6,000 Confederate and Union soldiers were dead and another 17,000 were seriously wounded. The Union had won the battle. Many people questioned the purpose of so much bloodshed.

Lincoln's Important Announcement

Five days after the Battle of Antietam, Lincoln issued the **Emancipation Proclamation**. This document stated that on January 1, 1863, all enslaved people in the Confederacy were emancipated, or freed. It did not apply to slave states that had stayed in the Union—Delaware, Kentucky, Maryland, and Missouri.

The Emancipation Proclamation was an executive order based on powers given to the President by the Constitution. Lincoln hoped it would give Union troops a new sense of purpose, weaken the South and, eventually, help the North win the war.

Public Opinion Changes

The Emancipation Proclamation changed ideas about the reasons for fighting the Civil War. Now the fighting was about more than Southern independence or saving the Union. It was also about slavery and freedom.

QUICK CHECK

Fact and Opinion What opinion do you think enslaved people had about the Emancipation Proclamation?

EVENT

Early in the Civil War, Lincoln's goal was to keep the Union together. Later he decided to use the **Emancipation Proclamation** to change public views and the course of the war.

The Emancipation Proclamation

THE WAR RAGES ON

Lincoln's Emancipation Proclamation encouraged thousands of free African Americans to join the Union army and navy. The Governor of Massachusetts asked an experienced officer and abolitionist, Robert Gould Shaw, to organize one of the first African American fighting forces.

The Fighting 54th

In February 1863 Shaw began training the 54th Massachusetts Colored Regiment at Camp Meigs, Massachusetts. This all-volunteer regiment included the two sons of Frederick Douglass. It became known as "The Fighting 54th."

On July 18, 1863, the 54th Regiment attacked Fort Wagner, South Carolina. Many men from the 54th died in the bloody fighting that ended in a Union defeat. In spite of the loss, the men of the Fighting 54th proved their bravery. Harriet Tubman, who helped care for the wounded, later described the battle:

❝And then we saw the lightning, and that was the guns; and then we heard the thunder, and that was the big guns; and then we heard the rain falling, and that was the drops of blood falling; and when we came to get the crops, it was dead men that we [gathered].❞

Although they were not treated as equals of white soldiers off the battlefield, they fought with courage in battle. By the end of the war, nearly 200,000 African Americans had joined the Union forces.

The Fighting 54th attacked Fort Wagner in South Carolina.

▲ Ulysses S. Grant watches his troops march into Vicksburg, Mississippi.

The Fall of Vicksburg

As you have read, one goal of the Anaconda Plan was for the Union to gain control of the Mississippi River. General Ulysses S. Grant achieved this goal in July 1863, when Union troops took control of Vicksburg, Mississippi.

For months, the city had been under siege by Grant's forces. In a siege, a military force surrounds a city and cuts it off. Grant's artillery pounded Vicksburg for weeks. Lack of food forced some people to eat rats! Finally the city fell on July 4, 1863. Grant was sickened by the sight of thousands of dead and wounded soldiers after the battle. Later, Grant wrote:

... after the battle ... one naturally [wants] to do as much to [stop] the suffering of an enemy as a friend.

—ULYSSES S. GRANT

The victory gave the Union control of the Mississippi River. More importantly for the Union, the Confederacy was now split in two. The Anaconda Plan was almost complete.

QUICK CHECK

Fact and Opinion How did Grant feel about people he had defeated after a battle?

269

By the spring of 1863, Lee's army had defeated the Union in several battles, including an important clash at Chancellorsville, Virginia. Unfortunately for the Confederates, General Stonewall Jackson was killed in the battle at Chancellorsville. This loss soon hurt the South. In June, Lee decided to take the war north again. His army marched through towns in southern Pennsylvania looking for badly needed supplies, especially shoes.

On July 1, 1863, Lee's army met Union troops under General George Meade in the small farm town of Gettysburg, Pennsylvania. Neither army had planned to fight there, but the nation would soon learn of the bloody Battle of Gettysburg. For two days, the armies fought each other. Ground was taken and lost, but neither side was able to win.

Pickett's Charge

On July 3, 1863, with the Confederate ammunition running low, Lee ordered General George Pickett to charge the Union lines. Confederate soldiers formed lines about a mile wide and half a mile deep. They began what came to be called "Pickett's Charge." More than 12,000 men ran almost one mile across an open field into cannon and rifle fire from Union troops. More than 6,000 men were killed and wounded in that attack. Lee was forced to retreat. The line of wagons carrying wounded soldiers back to Virginia was 17 miles long.

In all, about 51,000 soldiers were killed or wounded at the Battle of Gettysburg. It was the bloodiest battle ever fought in North America. Union victories at Gettysburg and Vicksburg turned the war in favor of the North.

▼ Thousands of Confederates died during Pickett's Charge. More than 51,000 men in all were killed or wounded at Gettysburg.

Confederate troops

Union troops

The Gettysburg Address

In November 1863, Lincoln gave a short speech at Gettysburg to dedicate a cemetery for dead Union soldiers. When he finished, the audience was silent. Lincoln thought his speech was a failure. But the people were silent out of respect for the powerful words.

The **Gettysburg Address** is known as one of the greatest speeches in American history. Read it in the Primary Sources feature.

QUICK CHECK

Fact and Opinion What was Lincoln's opinion of his speech at Gettysburg?

Primary Sources

The Gettysburg Address

"Four **score** and seven years ago our **fathers** brought forth on this continent, a new nation, **conceived** in liberty, and **dedicated** to the **proposition** that all men are created equal.

Now we are engaged in a great civil war, testing whether that nation, or any nation so conceived and so dedicated, can long endure. We are met on a great battlefield of that war. We have come to dedicate a portion of that field, as a final resting place for those who here gave their lives that that nation might live. It is altogether fitting and proper that we should do this.

But, in a larger sense, we cannot dedicate—we can not **consecrate**—we can not **hallow**—this ground. The brave men, living and dead, who struggled here, have consecrated it far above our poor power to add or detract. The world will little note nor long remember what we say here, but can never forget what they did here.

It is for us the living, rather, to be dedicated here to the unfinished work which they who fought here have thus far so nobly advanced. It is rather for us to be here dedicated to the great task remaining before us—that from these honored dead we take increased devotion to that cause for which they gave the last full measure of devotion; that we here highly resolve that these dead shall not have died in vain; that this nation, under God, shall have a new birth of freedom; and that government of the people, by the people, for the people, shall not perish from the earth."

by Abraham Lincoln • Gettysburg, Pennsylvania 1863

score: times twenty
fathers: forefathers or ancestors
conceived: formed
dedicated: set apart for a special purpose
proposition: intention or plan
consecrate: set apart as holy
hallow: consider holy

Write About It What reasons did Lincoln give for continuing the war?

An infantry camp

Rose Greenhow

A Civil War nurse

D THE WAR EFFORT

During the Civil War, civilians of all ages contributed to the war effort on both sides. Factory workers made weapons. Railroad workers transported troops and supplies. Even children played a role. Young people worked in family shops and helped on farms. Boys as young as 11 joined the army to serve as buglers or drummers. Men in their 60s and 70s signed up to fight. Others lied about their age to serve as soldiers.

Women and the War

Women in the North and South supported the war effort in many ways. On the home front, women worked in factories or ran family businesses while men were fighting in the war. They worked in shops, plowed fields, and harvested crops.

Women also helped the military. They cared for wounded soldiers, sewed uniforms, and made tents and ammunition. Some women took dangerous jobs as spies or nurses near the front lines. Rose Greenhow served as a Confederate spy. Before being caught, she directed a group of spies from her home in Washington, D.C. After getting information about Union plans, she sent coded messages

Harriet Tubman

A boy soldier

to the Confederate army. Greenhow also traveled to Europe to gain financial support for the South.

Harriet Tubman, the well-known conductor on the Underground Railroad, served the Union as a spy, scout, and nurse. Clara Barton served on the battlefied, bringing food, medicine, and supplies to the wounded. In 1881 she founded the American Red Cross.

QUICK CHECK

Fact and Opinion **Why did civilians help in the war effort?**

Check Understanding

1. **VOCABULARY** Write a paragraph about Abraham Lincoln using both vocabulary terms.

   Emancipation Proclamation
   Gettysburg Address

2. **READING SKILL** Fact and Opinion Use your chart from page 266 to write your opinion of the Gettysburg Address.

Fact	Opinion

3. **Write About It** Write about why you think men joined the Fighting 54th during the war.

EXPLORE The Big Idea

THE WAR ENDS

Lesson 5

VOCABULARY

malice p. 278

assassination p. 278

READING SKILL

Fact and Opinion

Copy the chart below. As you read, fill it in with facts and your own opinions about Sherman's March.

Fact	Opinion

STANDARDS FOCUS

SOCIAL STUDIES Time, Continuity, and Change

GEOGRAPHY The World in Spatial Terms

The Battle of Cold Harbor

Visual Preview

How did the end of the Civil War change the United States?

A General Grant sieged Richmond in order to capture the Confederate capital.

B Sherman marched through the South to bring an end to the Civil War.

C In April 1865, Richmond fell, Lee surrendered, and Lincoln was assassinated.

A THE FINAL BATTLES

Ulysses S. Grant was a strong general who had won important victories in the West. In 1864 Lincoln put Grant in command of the entire Union army. He hoped Grant would bring the war to an end.

Grant had two major goals. He wanted to destroy Lee's army in Virginia, and he wanted to capture Richmond, Virginia, the Confederate capital. For 40 days, from April to June 1864, he battled Lee's army.

The number of dead and wounded in these battles was enormous. At the Battle of Cold Harbor, Grant lost 7,000 men in about an hour. The Union army was so much larger than the Confederate army that it was able to continue its attacks. Finally, Grant reached Petersburg, a key railroad center south of Richmond. From there, he hoped to capture Richmond. Lee could not leave Petersburg. If he did, Grant would have a clear path to Richmond. With Lee trapped, Grant put Petersburg under siege for ten grim months.

People wondered if the war would ever end. Some Northerners wanted to let the Confederacy secede. Many blamed President Lincoln for continuing the fight to keep the Union together. As a result, Lincoln felt he had little hope of winning reelection in 1864.

QUICK CHECK

Fact and Opinion What opinion did some Northerners have about Lincoln's handling of the war?

▼ Richmond, Virginia, lay in ruins after the war.

B SHERMAN'S MARCH

General William Tecumseh Sherman led Union forces in the West. Following the Anaconda Plan, he marched his troops across Tennessee and Georgia to squeeze the South. He told his men to destroy anything of value to the enemy. Sherman's soldiers terrorized the South. They burned crops and buildings. They destroyed railroads and factories. They even killed livestock and left the animals for vultures. Sherman believed that the North needed to launch a total war, which would break the South's fighting spirit.

In September 1864, Sherman captured and burned Atlanta, Georgia, one of the South's

Battles of the Civil War

0   100   200 miles
0   100   200 kilometers

- Confederate states
- Union states
- Confederate victory
- Union victory
- Undecided battle
- Sherman's march
- General Sherman

Map Skill

DIRECTION **Where did General Sherman go after Savannah?**

largest cities and a railroad center. Sherman's 60,000-man army cut a 60-mile-wide and 300-mile-long path across Georgia to the city of Savannah on the Atlantic Coast. The Union force took Savannah in December. From there, the army marched into South Carolina—the state some people believed had started the war. Many cities in Sherman's path were left in ashes. One soldier said:

> **❝**Here is where treason began and . . . here is where it shall end!**❞**

With the fall of Atlanta, it seemed the end of the war was finally in sight. Northerners began to regain confidence in Lincoln and his ability to lead the Union to victory. In November 1864, voters reelected him. See the the results of the election in the datagraphic on this page.

QUICK CHECK

Fact and Opinion What opinion did many Northern soldiers have about South Carolina?

▼ Union troops destroyed many parts of the South during Sherman's March.

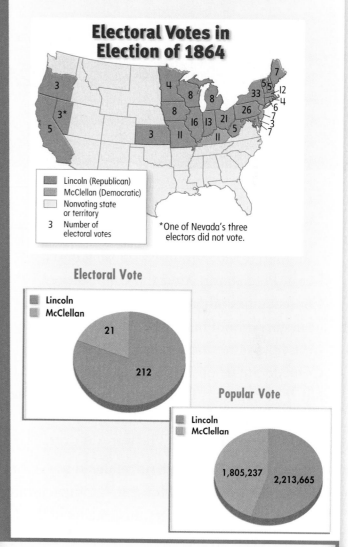

DataGraphic
The Election of 1864

In 1864 the Democratic nominee for President, George McClellan, ran against Abraham Lincoln. Use the map and the graphs to answer the questions about the election of 1864.

Electoral Votes in Election of 1864

3
4
8 8
33
7
5 5
12
4
8
26
6
4
3*
16 13 21
7
3
5 3 11 5
7
11

- ■ Lincoln (Republican)
- ■ McClellan (Democratic)
- ☐ Nonvoting state or territory
- 3 Number of electoral votes

*One of Nevada's three electors did not vote.

Electoral Vote

- ■ Lincoln
- ■ McClellan

21
212

Popular Vote

- ■ Lincoln
- ■ McClellan

1,805,237 2,213,665

Think About the 1864 Election

1. What states did McClellan win?
2. Why was the popular vote much closer than the electoral vote?

277

Robert E. Lee surrendered to Ulysses S. Grant at Appomattox Court House in Virginia.

ⓒ THE SOUTH SURRENDERS

In March 1865 Grant was closing in on Lee at Petersburg. After the Union siege, Confederate soldiers defending the city were near starvation. On April 2, Lee took his army west, hoping to find food and gather more Confederate troops. As a result, Petersburg fell. The next day, Richmond, the Confederate capital, also fell. Lee knew that more killing would be meaningless. The war was over.

On April 9, 1865, Lee surrendered to Grant at Appomattox Court House in Virginia. Grant did not take any prisoners. Instead, he offered Lee generous terms. For example, Lee and his soldiers were allowed to return to their homes. They could also keep their horses to help with the spring plowing.

After Lee's surrender, Jefferson Davis fled westward, where he hoped to keep the Confederacy alive. On May 10, 1865, he was captured by Union soldiers. Davis was later imprisoned for two years in Virginia.

Lincoln Is Shot

Lincoln did not want to punish the South. In his second inaugural address, he encouraged Americans to put away their **malice**, or desire to harm, with these words: "With malice toward none, with charity for all."

Less than a week after Lee's surrender, Lincoln was watching a play at Ford's Theater in Washington, D.C. Suddenly a gunshot rang out. John Wilkes Booth had shot the President. The next morning, April 15, 1865, Lincoln died. Abraham Lincoln's **assassination** shocked the nation. Assassination is the murder of an important leader. The poet Walt Whitman expressed the country's sadness:

O CAPTAIN! my Captain! our fearful trip is done; The ship has weather'd every [storm], the prize we sought is won;

—WALT WHITMAN

Troops Return Home

At the end of the war, the South had few farms left in working condition. Troops returned not only to the property that had been destroyed, but to a way of life that had ended. In the South, one of every four white men had been killed. Two-thirds of its wealth had been lost. It would take many years for the South to recover. One Confederate soldier, returning home to Richmond, wrote:

> **"**I shall not attempt to describe my feelings. The city [is] in ruins. . . . With a raging headache and a swelling heart I reach my home, and here the curtain falls.**"**

The Union had survived, but the cost of the Civil War had been huge. The North's victory ended slavery for millions of African Americans. At the same time, it left the South in ruins. United once again, the nation faced the task of rebuilding the South.

QUICK CHECK

Fact and Opinion Why did Lincoln say he would show "malice toward none"?

Check Understanding

1. **VOCABULARY** Write a paragraph about Abraham Lincoln using both vocabulary words.

   malice   **assassination**

2. **READING SKILL** **Fact and Opinion** Use your chart from page 274 to help you write about Sherman's March.

Fact	Opinion

3. **EXPLORE The Big Idea** **Write About It** Why did most Northern voters support Lincoln and want to continue the war?

▼ Abraham Lincoln's funeral procession passed through several states on its way to Springfield, Illinois.

279

Lesson 6

RECONSTRUCTION AND AFTER

VOCABULARY

Reconstruction p. 281

black codes p. 281

sharecropping p. 282

segregation p. 285

Jim Crow laws p. 285

READING SKILL

Fact and Opinion

Copy the chart below. As you read, fill it in with facts about Reconstruction and the opinions people had about Reconstruction.

Fact	Opinion

STANDARDS FOCUS

SOCIAL STUDIES Power, Authority, and Governance

GEOGRAPHY Places and Regions

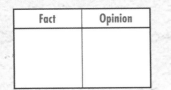

The Freedmen's Bureau started schools such as this one in Charleston, South Carolina.

Visual Preview

How did the South change after the war?

A The Freedmen's Bureau provided valuable services to help blacks and whites.

B Amendments to the Constitution gave people more rights, but life was still difficult.

C Southern states began a policy of segregation after Reconstruction ended.

A   REBUILDING THE SOUTH

After the Civil War, President Lincoln wanted to end the harsh feelings between the North and South. Before letting the defeated Confederate states back into the Union, he asked them to take an oath to support the Constitution and the Union.

Before his death, Lincoln created a plan for **Reconstruction**, or rebuilding the South. In March 1865, he had signed a bill that created the Freedmen's Bureau. This government program was part of Reconstruction. It provided food, clothing, shelter, medical care, jobs, and legal help to both African Americans and whites. It also set up 4,000 schools for newly freed people.

African Americans also set up schools. By 1870 African Americans had spent over $1 million on education. Several colleges and universities for African Americans were founded in the South. Among these were Fisk University in Tennessee and Spelman College in Georgia.

Congress and President Andrew Johnson supported the Freedmen's Bureau. But they clashed over who would control other parts of Reconstruction.

Johnson Is Impeached

Few Presidents have been more unpopular than Andrew Johnson. Southerners disliked him because he had supported the Union. Northerners disliked him because he allowed former Confederate leaders to serve in Congress.

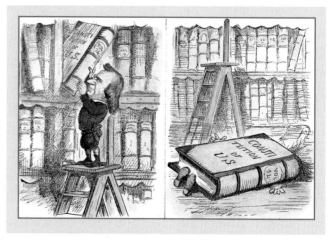

▲ This political cartoon criticizing President Andrew Johnson shows him being crushed the by U.S. Constitution.

He also took no action when Southern states passed **black codes**, laws that restricted the rights of African Americans.

The House of Representatives voted to impeach Johnson. To impeach is to charge an official with wrongdoing. If two-thirds of the 36 Senators had voted against Johnson, he would have been removed from office. The vote was 35 to 19. He remained in office, but the division between the North and South also remained.

QUICK CHECK

Fact and Opinion **What opinion did many in the South have about Andrew Johnson?**

281

After two years of struggling with President Johnson over who would control Reconstruction, Congress passed the first Reconstruction Act in 1867. This act divided the South into five districts. The districts would remain under the control of the U.S. Army until new governments could be formed. Each state had to write a new constitution.

Amendments to the Constitution

Before Lincoln's death in 1865, Congress approved the Thirteenth Amendment. This amendment abolished slavery. During Reconstruction, a Southern state had to ratify the Thirteenth Amendment in order to return to the Union. Other amendments that passed after Lincoln's death guaranteed rights to African Americans. In 1868 the Fourteenth Amendment made African Americans citizens of the United States and guaranteed them the same legal rights as whites. In 1870 the Fifteenth Amendment made it illegal for states to deny a man's right to vote. Women were not included in the amendment.

A New Way of Life

After the Civil War, most plantation owners had little money to pay workers. Instead, they rented out their fields. Landowners usually accepted part of the crop grown on their land as rent—sometimes as much as one-half of the crop. This system of renting land in return for a share of the crop raised on it is called **sharecropping**. It sounds fair, but most people who worked in the fields remained poor.

They did not make much money because the price for cotton was low. Many farmers had to borrow money to survive. By doing this, they slipped deeply into debt.

Citizenship
Rights and Responsibilities

As an American citizen, you have the responsibility to protect not only your own rights but the rights of others. Suppose you were asked to attend a meeting to suggest rules for the playground. You have a right to speak and give your suggestions. You also have a responsibility to be careful about what you say and to respect the ideas of others.

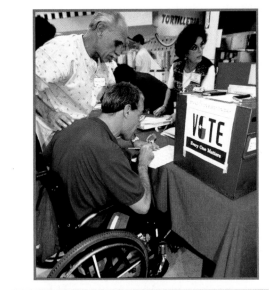

Write About It Explain the responsibilities citizens have when voting and what might happen if people were not allowed to vote.

Northerners in the South

At the same time, many Northerners moved to the South to start businesses. They soon became active in the fight for African Americans' rights. Southerners often called these Northerners "carpetbaggers" because many carried suitcases made of carpeting. Many Southerners believed that carpetbaggers were taking advantage of the South's suffering. Many carpetbaggers were former Union soldiers or members of the Freedmen's Bureau who wanted to settle in the South.

QUICK CHECK

Fact and Opinion What opinion did Southerners have about carpetbaggers?

▼ This newspaper cartoon shows a carpetbagger from the North. What was the cartoonist's opinion of carpetbaggers?

▼ A family of sharecroppers in Virginia in 1899

▲ Hiram R. Revels (left) and Blanche K. Bruce (right)

ⓒ RECONSTRUCTION ENDS

During Reconstruction, more than 600 African Americans were elected to state office and 16 were elected to Congress. Among them were Hiram R. Revels and Blanche K. Bruce from Mississippi, who were both elected to the United States Senate. Some Southern whites were not ready to accept and treat African Americans as equals.

Violence in the South

Many white Southerners didn't want African Americans to hold public office. They did not want to pay higher taxes for schools and roads that helped African Americans. Some Southerners turned to violence to terrorize African Americans and their white supporters.

In 1866 six former Confederate officers formed the Ku Klux Klan. Disguised in white robes and hoods, they terrorized African Americans, driving them from their homes and destroying their property. They used "night raids" and murder to keep African Americans from voting. African Americans working for whites were often told they would be fired

▼ The Ku Klux Klan terrorized African Americans.

if they voted. Sometimes whites kept the locations of voting places secret from African American voters. In some places, African Americans were forced to pay an illegal "poll tax" in order to vote. Many people could not afford to pay the tax.

Jim Crow Laws

In the presidential election of 1876, Democrat Samuel J. Tilden of New York won the popular vote. The electoral vote, however, was in question in some states, including three in the South. The Republican candidate, Rutherford B. Hayes, promised to remove all Union troops from the South if the electoral votes were cast for him. The Democrats from the South, who were white, voted for the Republican in order to end Reconstruction.

President Hayes quickly ordered the removal of federal troops, bringing an end to Reconstruction. After federal troops left, Southern states began a policy called **segregation**. Segregation is the separation of people based on race. The **Jim Crow laws** made segregation legal in the South. Under the Jim Crow laws, blacks and whites could not use the same schools, restaurants, railroad cars, hotels, or parks. In 1896 the Supreme Court in *Plessy* v. *Ferguson* ruled that "separate but equal"

services were Constitutional. In reality, such services were rarely equal.

In the late 1800s, African Americans experienced discrimination in the North as well as the South. African Americans in the North were often not allowed in many public places. Although Reconstruction granted equal citizenship, segregation resulted in unequal treatment. African Americans did not gain many of the rights guaranteed by the Thirteenth, Fourteenth, and Fifteenth Amendments until the Civil Rights movement of the 1950s and 1960s.

QUICK CHECK

Fact and Opinion **How did the decision in *Plessy* v. *Ferguson* hurt African Americans?**

Check Understanding

1. **VOCABULARY** Write a paragraph about African Americans after the Civil War using these vocabulary terms.

Reconstruction	sharecropping
black codes	segregation

2. **READING SKILL** Fact and Opinion Use your chart from page 280 to write an opinion about Reconstruction.

Fact	Opinion

3. **Write About It** Write about the ways African Americans improved their lives in the South.

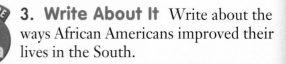

285

Vocabulary

Number a paper from 1 to 4. Beside each number, write the word from the list that matches the description.

blockade   black codes

malice   segregation

1. The separation of people based on race

2. The closing of an area to keep supplies from moving

3. Laws passed by the Southern states that limited the rights of the African Americans

4. The desire to harm someone

Comprehension and Critical Thinking

5. How did Harriet Tubman help enslaved Africans?

6. **Reading Skill** Identify one fact and one opinion about carpetbaggers.

7. **Critical Thinking** Why did Sherman believe that only total war would lead to a Union victory?

8. **Critical Thinking** In what ways was Reconstruction unsuccessful in improving the lives of African Americans?

Skill

Use Climographs

Write a complete sentence to answer each question.

9. Which are Richmond's two driest months?

10. How would you describe Richmond's temperature during the wettest month of the year?

Richmond, Virginia

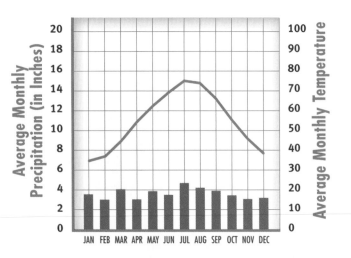

Test Preparation

Read the passage. Then answer the questions.

During the Civil War, the Union had several advantages over the Confederacy. The North had a larger population and more workers, as well as greater factory and textile production. It had more farmland, more miles of railroad, and more ships. It could feed, arm, and move a large army more easily.

The Confederacy also had some advantages. Southerners were fighting for their way of life. The army fought on familiar land and had officers with years of military experience. One of them, Robert E. Lee, became commander of the Confederate army.

1. What is the main idea of the passage?

A. The Union was better suited for a long, costly war.

B. Both the Union and the Confederacy had advantages in the Civil War.

C. The Union could feed, arm, and move a large army.

D. General Lee helped win the war.

2. Which statement best summarizes the Union's advantages?

A. Fighting for independence

B. Larger army with better supplies

C. Fighting for their way of life

D. Leaders with battle experience

3. What was one difference between the Union and the Confederacy?

A. The Confederacy fought on familiar land, while the Union did not.

B. The Union had experienced officers, while the Confederacy did not.

C. The Union had Robert E. Lee, while the Confederacy did not.

D. The Confederacy could feed a large army, while the Union could not.

4. Why did Robert E. Lee join the Confederacy?

5. What advantages would an army have if soldiers were fighting to protect their way of life?

The Big Idea Activities

What are some things people are willing to fight for?

Write About the Big Idea

Expository Essay
Use the Unit 6 Foldable to help you write an expository essay that answers the Big Idea question, *What are some things people are willing to fight for*? Use the Notes you wrote under each tab in the Foldable for details to support each main idea. Be sure to begin with an introduction that includes facts. Include one paragraph that explains the reason for each fact. End with a concluding paragraph that includes your opinion.

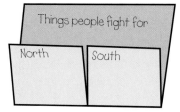

Make a Poster

Make a poster of a person or event you read about in Unit 6. Here's how to make your poster.

1. Find or draw a picture of the person's face, the person in action, or the event you chose.

2. Research the person or event you chose to find five interesting facts.

3. Use resources available from your library or historical sites on the Internet.

Illustrate your poster with drawings of some of the interesting facts.

Frederick Douglass

1. Douglass escaped slavery

2. Gave a speech at the . . .

3. Became publisher of several abolitionist newspapers

4. Best-selling autobiography

5. Gave a speech at Lincoln's memorial

The Nation Grows

Factory workers in a steel mill.

Unit 7

Essential Question
How does technology change people's lives?

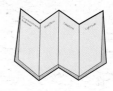

Summarize
Make and label a four-tab Foldable book before you read this unit. Label the four sections **Transcontinental Railroad**, **Steel Plow**, **Telephone**, and **Lightbulb**. Use the Foldable to organize information as you read.

For more about Unit 7 go to www.macmillanmh.com

PEOPLE, PLACES, AND EVENTS

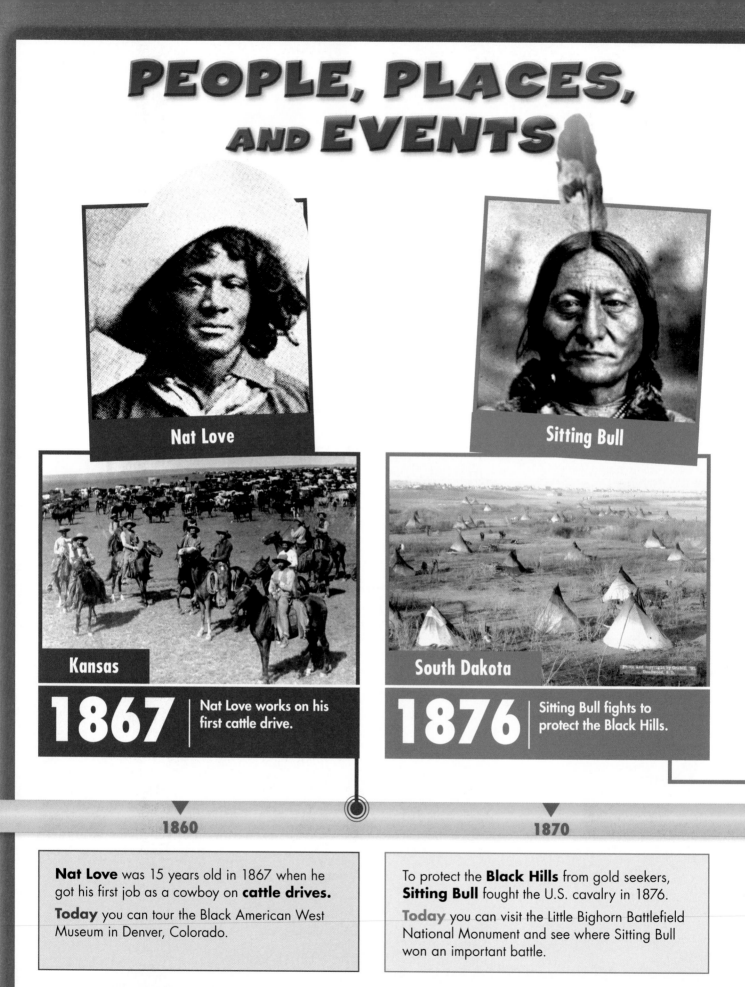

Nat Love

Sitting Bull

Kansas

South Dakota

1867 | Nat Love works on his first cattle drive.

1876 | Sitting Bull fights to protect the Black Hills.

1860

1870

Nat Love was 15 years old in 1867 when he got his first job as a cowboy on **cattle drives.**

Today you can tour the Black American West Museum in Denver, Colorado.

To protect the **Black Hills** from gold seekers, **Sitting Bull** fought the U.S. cavalry in 1876.

Today you can visit the Little Bighorn Battlefield National Monument and see where Sitting Bull won an important battle.

For more about People, Places, and Events, visit
www.macmillanmh.com

Thomas Edison

New Jersey

1879 | Thomas Edison develops first electric lightbulb.

Jane Addams

Illinois

1889 | Jane Addams founds Hull House in Chicago.

1880

1890

In 1879 **Thomas Edison** developed the first **electric lightbulb** in his laboratory.

Today you can see the Thomas Edison Museum in Edison, New Jersey.

In 1889 **Jane Addams** founded **Hull House** in Chicago, Illinois, to help immigrants in their new lives in the United States.

Today you can visit the Hull House Museum in Chicago.

SETTLING THE WEST

VOCABULARY

cattle drive p. 293

transcontinental railroad p. 294

homesteader p. 296

exodusters p. 297

poverty p. 297

READING SKILL

Summarize

Copy the chart below. Use it to summarize the inventions that changed American life in the West.

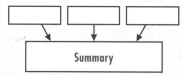

Summary

STANDARDS FOCUS

SOCIAL STUDIES People, Places, and Environments

GEOGRAPHY Places and Regions

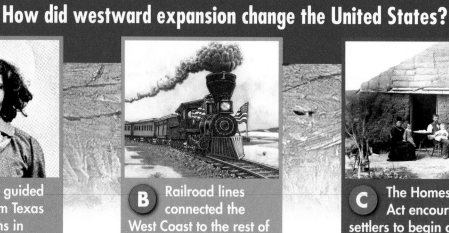

Cowboys rode well-trained horses and used ropes called lariats to herd cattle on long drives.

Visual Preview

How did westward expansion change the United States?

A Cowboys guided cattle from Texas to railroad towns in Kansas.

B Railroad lines connected the West Coast to the rest of the country.

C The Homestead Act encouraged settlers to begin a new life on the Great Plains.

Ⓐ THE CATTLE KINGDOM

Cattle ranchers in Texas raised millions of cattle on the open ranges. The best place to sell the cattle was in the North. How did cowboys get all those cattle to markets thousands of miles away?

Cowboys went on long journeys, called **cattle drives**, to guide cattle from Texas ranches to the railroads in Kansas. From there, the animals could be shipped east by train. In most cases, the cattle were sent to Chicago, Illinois, where they were prepared for sale.

Cowboy Life

Cowboys spent months on the trail, traveling hundreds of miles. They faced bad weather, cattle stampedes, dangerous river crossings, and occasional attacks from Native Americans. Nat Love was a well-known African American ranch hand. According to Nat Love:

> **❝**The test of a cowboy's worth is his ... nerve. He is not supposed to know what fear means, and I assure you there are very few who know the meaning of that word.**❞**

The End of Cattle Drives

Sometimes cattle drives faced more than bad weather or attacks from Native Americans. Many farmers refused to let cattle cross their lands. Some states passed laws preventing cattle from crossing state borders. Since railroads had begun to reach south into Texas by the late 1800s, ranchers soon began shipping their cattle by train directly to Chicago from railyards near their ranches.

QUICK CHECK

Summarize **Why did the cattle drives end?**

Nat Love went on his first cattle drive at age 15.

THE TRANSCONTINENTAL RAILROAD

After the 1848 discovery of gold in California, there was greater need for a **transcontinental railroad**, or a railroad that crosses the continent. Congress passed the Pacific Railway Act in 1862 granting two railroad companies land to build the railroad.

Congress added amendments that offered money and land for every mile completed.

From the start, building the railroad proved difficult, because many workers were fighting in the Civil War. By 1865 neither company had laid more than 50 miles of track.

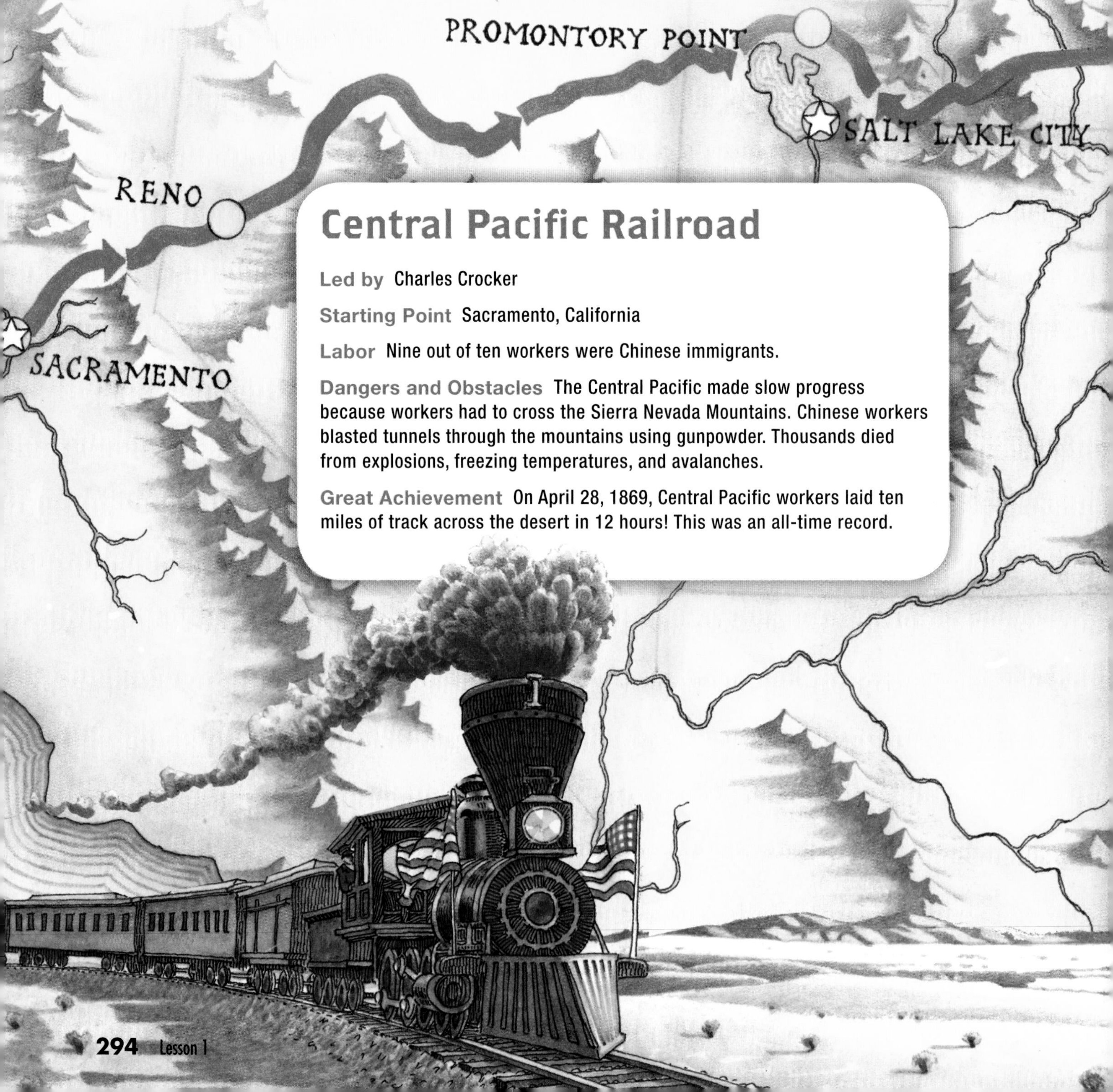

PROMONTORY POINT

SALT LAKE CITY

RENO

SACRAMENTO

Central Pacific Railroad

Led by Charles Crocker

Starting Point Sacramento, California

Labor Nine out of ten workers were Chinese immigrants.

Dangers and Obstacles The Central Pacific made slow progress because workers had to cross the Sierra Nevada Mountains. Chinese workers blasted tunnels through the mountains using gunpowder. Thousands died from explosions, freezing temperatures, and avalanches.

Great Achievement On April 28, 1869, Central Pacific workers laid ten miles of track across the desert in 12 hours! This was an all-time record.

The Golden Spike

Finally, after six years, the Union Pacific and the Central Pacific railways met at Promontory Point, Utah. The tracks were joined by a spike made of gold. Five days later, train service began. Ticket prices were $111 for first class, $80 for second class, and $40 for third class.

The trip was uncomfortable, but now it took one week instead of many months to travel from New York to San Francisco.

QUICK CHECK

Summarize **Why did the Central Pacific Railroad make slower progress than the Union Pacific?**

LARAMIE

CHEYENNE

OMAHA

Union Pacific Railroad

Lead by Grenville Dodge

Starting Point Omaha, Nebraska

Labor Many were Irish and German immigrants who were paid low wages but received food and shelter.

Dangers and Obstacles Work was easier on the Union Pacific Railroad because track was built across the Great Plains. The Lakota and Cheyenne often attacked the railroad workers, because the tracks were cutting across their traditional hunting grounds. The Union Pacific began to post soldiers along the track as the railroad continued west.

Great Achievement Grenville Dodge had been a general in the Union Army. He organized his work teams like army units. They were able to lay track more quickly than the Central Pacific Railroad.

GREAT AMERICAN
OVERLAND ROUTE
TO THE
UNITED STATES
AND
EUROPE,
VIA THE
Central AND Union
PACIFIC
RAIL ROAD LINE.
TO
BALTIMORE, NEW YORK,
PHILADELPHIA, and BOSTON,
AND
ATLANTIC STEAMERS TO LIVERPOOL
AND ALL OTHER PRINCIPAL SEAPORTS OF EUROPE.
THROUGH TICKETS
For Sale at the Agencies of the Trans-Pacific Steamship Lines, and at the
THROUGH FREIGHT AND TICKET OFFICE,
NEW MONTGOMERY STREET, SAN FRANCISCO.
THROUGH EXPRESS AND MAIL TRAINS
THROUGH TIME, SIX DAYS AND TWENTY HOURS.
Silver Palace Sleeping Coaches

JOHN CORNING,   T. H. GOODMAN,   A. N. TOWNE,

HOMESTEADING ON THE PLAINS

For many years, people thought that farming was impossible in the dry region called the Great Plains. Then, in 1862, President Lincoln signed the Homestead Act. Under this act, a head of a household who was at least 21 years old could claim a 160-acre piece of land and had to pay a fee of only $26. People who claimed land under this act became known as **homesteaders**. Eventually, 270 million acres, about 10 percent of the area of the United States, was settled under the Homestead Act.

Life on the Plains

Life was hard for homesteaders. There were few trees for lumber and little water on the plains. In the cold winters, bitter winds whipped snow into drifts high enough to cover houses. Summer very often brought prairie fires, droughts, and locusts to the plains.

Even the land itself seemed to fight the new settlers. They called themselves sodbusters because of the tough ground, called sod, they had to break through to plant crops. Because there were no trees for wood, homesteaders made soddies, or houses built out of the sod they removed. They also used tough prairie grass to strengthen walls and roofs.

Farming the plains became a little easier in the mid–1800's, when Scottish immigrant James Oliver invented the chilled-steel plow. This new plow would not crack or break if it hit a stone.

▼ Homesteaders built homes from sod, the grass and soil that covered the Great Plains.

▼ This photograph shows Washington Street in Nicodemus, Kansas, a town settled by exodusters.

African American Settlers

After Reconstruction ended in 1877, many African Americans felt that the only way to be truly free was to leave the South. The end of Reconstruction also meant the end of federal protection for African Americans in the south. Henry Adams, an African American leader from Louisiana, encouraged African Americans to move to Kansas. People who followed Adams's advice called themselves **exodusters**. An exodus is a journey to freedom.

Thousands of black families from the South joined what became known as the Kansas Fever Exodus. Many exodusters faced hard times and **poverty**, or lack of money and property, just as they had in the South. Despite these hardships, Kansas's black population continued to grow.

QUICK CHECK

Summarize **Why did African Americans decide to leave the South and move to Kansas?**

Check Understanding

1. **VOCABULARY** Write a paragraph explaining the difference between these two vocabulary terms.

   homesteaders   exodusters

2. **READING SKILL** Summarize Use the chart from page 292 to write a paragraph that summarizes the building of the transcontinental railroad.

3. **Write About It** Explain how the chilled-steel plow helped homesteaders farm the plains.

The Plains Wars

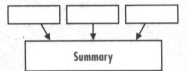

VOCABULARY

property rights p. 299

reservation p. 299

READING SKILL

Summarize

Copy the chart below. Use it to summarize details about the Plains Wars.

Summary

STANDARDS FOCUS

SOCIAL STUDIES Power, Authority, and Governance

GEOGRAPHY Human Systems

Custer is defeated at the Battle of the Little Bighorn.

Visual Preview

How did growth in the West affect Native American groups?

A Settlers killed the buffalo and forced Native Americans to live on reservations.

B Native Americans were often forced off their lands as a result of the Plains Wars.

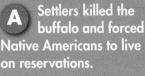

NATIVE AMERICAN LANDS

A brown ocean of buffalo once covered Native American lands. When the settlers and railroads came, the buffalo disappeared. The Native Americans' way of life was threatened.

The Homestead Act, which you have read about, gave settlers on the Great Plains **property rights** to the land. Property rights are the rights to own or use something for sale. Some Native American groups did not believe that land could belong to a person or that it could be sold. These different views of land and property led to majors conflicts.

Losing a Way of Life

Native American groups, such as the Lakota and Cheyenne, had been hunting buffalo on the Great Plains for centuries. These large animals were the most important part of Native American life on the Great Plains. They provided food, shelter, tools, and clothing. Before settlers and railroads arrived, around 50 million buffalo roamed the Great Plains. Over a period of about 40 years, settlers and railroad workers killed most of the huge animals. By 1900, fewer than 1,000 buffalo were left.

In the 1860s settlers and Native Americans fought over land. The United States government moved Native Americans to **reservations** to make more land available for settlers and railroads.

A reservation is land set aside for a Native American group or groups.

Native Americans felt they had to fight for their way of life or it would be lost forever. The clashes between Native Americans and settlers during this period of westward expansion are called the Plains Wars.

QUICK CHECK

Summarize **Why did the United States government move Native Americans to reservations?**

▲ The buffalo was an important natural resource.

299

In 1868 the United States signed a treaty with the Lakota, granting them large areas of land. The grant included the Black Hills area of present-day South Dakota. This area had deep religious meaning to the Lakota. Then, in 1874, gold was discovered in the Black Hills. Immediately, thousands of miners flooded into this sacred part of the Lakota territory. Violence quickly followed.

▲ General George Custer

Little Bighorn

The Lakota chiefs, including Sitting Bull and Crazy Horse, refused to allow miners to dig in the Black Hills. As a result, U.S. soldiers were sent to drive Sitting Bull and the Lakota out of the area and onto reservations.

On June 25, 1876, Colonel George Custer attacked Sitting Bull's camp on the Little Bighorn River. Too late, Custer discovered that he was outnumbered four to one. Hundreds of Lakota warriors counter attacked, killing Custer and all of his troops at the Battle of Little Bighorn. It was the last major Native American victory on the Great Plains.

March of the Nez Perce

Fighting between the army and Native Americans soon reached the Northwest region. In 1877 Chief Joseph and the Nez Perce began a 1,200-mile march from eastern Oregon to Canada. They were trying to avoid being forced onto a reservation. Only 40 miles from Canada, the Nez Perce encountered a force of 500 American soldiers. Cold and hungry, the Nez Perce held out for five days. Finally, Chief Joseph surrendered on October 5, 1877.

Wounded Knee

After moving to a reservation in South Dakota, the Sioux performed a ritual to express

◀ Chief Joseph surrendered after many of his people were killed.

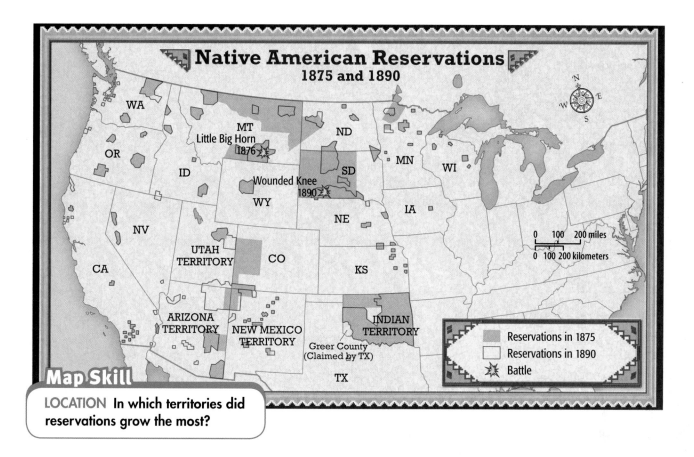

Native American Reservations
1875 and 1890

WA
OR
ID
NV
CA
MT
Little Big Horn 1876
WY
UTAH TERRITORY
ARIZONA TERRITORY
ND
SD
Wounded Knee 1890
NE
CO
NEW MEXICO TERRITORY
MN
WI
IA
KS
Greer County (Claimed by TX)
INDIAN TERRITORY
TX

0   100   200 miles
0   100 200 kilometers

Reservations in 1875
Reservations in 1890
Battle

Map Skill

LOCATION **In which territories did reservations grow the most?**

the destruction of their culture. The ritual spread and was banned by reservation officials. To stop the ritual, officials attempted to arrest their chief, Sitting Bull. In the scuffle, Sitting Bull was shot. Hundreds of Sioux fled fearing for their lives. The army soon arrived to collect the Sioux's weapons. Shots rang out again, killing more than 200 Sioux and 25 soldiers.

Native American Losses

Despite the loss of traditional lands, Native Americans continued to fight for their rights. Although their way of life has changed since the late 1800s, Native American groups have kept their traditions alive. Traditional clothing, dances, and stories preserve the history of the Plains groups.

QUICK CHECK

Summarize **Why were the Lakota willing to fight for the Black Hills?**

Check Understanding

1. **VOCABULARY** Write a paragraph about the Plains Wars using the vocabulary words below.

   property rights   **reservation**

2. **READING SKILL** Summarize Use the chart from page 298 to summarize the Plains Wars.

   Summary

3. **Write About It** Write a paragraph explaining how the railroads changed life for Plains groups.

BIG BUSINESS

VOCABULARY

corporation p. 304

monopoly p. 304

labor union p. 305

strike p. 305

READING SKILL

Summarize
Copy the chart below. Use it to summarize the inventions that changed American life in the late 1800s.

Summary

STANDARDS FOCUS

SOCIAL STUDIES Science, Technology, and Society

GEOGRAPHY Environment and Society

The 1893 World's Columbian Exposition in Chicago, Illinois, introduced electricity to millions of people.

Visual Preview

How did technology affect American life in the late 1800s?

A American inventors led the United States into the modern industrial age.

B As corporation owners grew wealthy, workers demanded better working conditions.

302

Ⓐ WORLD'S INVENTION CAPITAL

On New Year's Eve in 1879, crowds poured into Menlo Park, New Jersey. They packed the boardwalk outside the laboratory of inventor Thomas Edison to see the world's first electric lights.

Edison's electric light proved something that most Americans already believed—the United States was the world's most modern country. In the late 1800s, elevators, telephones, and other inventions changed American life forever.

Time of Inventions

In the late 1800s, inventors were seen as heroes, similar to how explorers had been viewed in the past. Edison was known as the "Wizard of Menlo Park." He admitted, however, that his success had little to do with magic. For him, success came from hard work. He said,

> **"Genius is 1 percent inspiration and 99 percent perspiration."**

Edison and his assistants eventually developed more than 1,000 inventions. Besides the electric light, he made the first machine to record sound in 1877, which became the phonograph. He also made the first moving picture projector in 1896.

In 1876 Edison worked around the clock to develop another invention—the telephone. But Alexander Graham Bell, a teacher of people who were deaf, invented it first. Bell's interest in

Lewis Lattimer

communication led him to explore ways to send sound over electrical wires.

Both Bell and Edison had help from a valuable assistant. Lewis Lattimer, an African American scientist, helped design the first telephone with Alexander Graham Bell. Later, working for Thomas Edison, Lattimer developed a longer lasting electric light bulb. Lattimer's light bulb had a filament—the part that glows—made of carbon instead of paper. This made bulbs last longer and brought electric lighting into homes.

QUICK CHECK

Summarize Why did people believe the United States was the world's most modern country?

303

To reach American homes, these new inventions had to be made in large numbers, then shipped, and sold. People established **corporations** for this purpose. A corporation is a large company in which people invest money and share ownership. Two of the largest corporations were based on the building and transportation industries—steel and oil.

Carnegie Steel Company

Andrew Carnegie came to the United States from Scotland at age 12 in 1848. By the time he was in his thirties, he owned steel plants in Pittsburgh, Pennsylvania. Railroads used steel for tracks and cars. Steel was also used for bridges and skyscrapers. Carnegie's plants made steel faster than those of his competitors.

Rockefeller and Standard Oil

Oil was an important industry long before it was used in cars as gasoline. In 1858 a miner struck oil in Pennsylvania. The black liquid was made into kerosene for lamps. Soon it greased the moving parts of industrial machines and railroad locomotives.

In 1870 John D. Rockefeller formed the Standard Oil Company. He bought plants that turned crude oil into kerosene. He also purchased several railways and forced them to carry only his kerosene. By 1885 Rockefeller controlled the U.S. oil industry.

Standard Oil, similar to Carnegie Steel, became a **monopoly**. A monopoly is a business that completely controls an industry.

▼ In 1894 the Pullman strike in Chicago, Illinois, stopped railroad traffic in the West. The strike led to riots and federal troops were called in.

Most Americans believed that the only way to have fair prices was for businesses to compete. While owners grew rich, workers struggled.

Workers Join Together

In 1900 the average laborer worked a 60-hour week. Workers typically earned about $400 a year. A family of four needed at least $800 to survive. Working conditions were usually dirty and dangerous. Textile workers breathed air filled with tiny fibers that caused lung problems. Miners risked death from underground explosions. A factory in Connecticut had 16,000 accidents in one year.

Workers wanted better conditions, but they had little power when they acted alone. To protect themselves, workers formed **labor unions**—groups that represented workers. In 1886 the American Federation of Labor, or AFL, was founded by Samuel Gompers. The AFL represented many unions. Its

leaders pushed for higher pay for all workers, workplace safety, and an eight-hour workday.

Industries that refused union demands could face a **strike**, when workers refuse to work. A strike could cost an industry millions of dollars. Employers often used violence against strikers for that reason. In 1892 a strike at Carnegie's Homestead Steel plant caused a gun battle between workers and security men. It killed ten people. Labor unions won small battles in the 1800s. During this time, most workers had little power against large corporations.

QUICK CHECK

Summarize **Why did workers form labor unions?**

Check Understanding

1. **VOCABULARY** Write one sentence using two of the vocabulary words about how workers fought for better conditions.

   monopoly   labor union   strike

2. **READING SKILL** Summarize Use the chart from page 302 to explain why corporations were important in the late 1800s.

3. **Write About It** Briefly describe how electric lighting changed people's way of life.

▲ Samuel Gompers, bottom right, founded the American Federation of Labor. By 1914, the AFL had two million members.

305

Growing Cities

Lesson 4

VOCABULARY

commute p. 307

slum p. 308

tenement p. 308

READING SKILL

Summarize

Copy the chart below. Use it to write a summary about the growth of cities.

```
[  ]   [  ]   [  ]
   ↓     ↓     ↓
     Summary
```

STANDARDS FOCUS

SOCIAL STUDIES — People, Places, and Environments

GEOGRAPHY — Environment and Society

Elevated trains in New York City carried people to work. In the late 1800s, cities became the center of American life.

Visual Preview

How did the growth of cities impact the United States?

A U.S. cities grew rapidly as people moved from farms to work in industry.

B Immigrants from Asia and Europe arrived in the United States.

C Anti-immigrant feelings led to laws that stopped most immigration.

AMERICANS MOVE TO CITIES

In 1860 fewer than one in five Americans lived in communities larger than 8,000 people. By 1920 more than half of all Americans lived in urban, or city, areas.

New cities had growing pains—sewage in the streets, overcrowded buildings, and crime. Cities, however, were the centers of the industrial age. Many people moved to cities in search of work.

The Changing City

Many cities grew up around a single industry. Minneapolis milled flour and Milwaukee brewed beer. New England cities manufactured clothes and shoes. Chicago, St. Louis, and Denver became railroad centers where produce, goods, and people moved in and out in great clouds of locomotive steam.

Fast-growing cities such as Chicago, New York, and St. Louis created markets for American inventions and industry. These cities needed Carnegie's steel for buildings and Edison's lights for streets, homes, and businesses.

New technology brought other changes to daily life in cities. In crowded cities, waste collected fast. City planners tried to solve the problem with indoor plumbing that carried waste and water to underground sewage pipes.

Many city officials also had to solve transportation problems. Workers had to **commute**, or travel to their jobs. In the 1890s Chicago and New York established the first electric streetcar system. Boston moved its transportation underground. In 1897 the first subway system in the United States opened in Boston, Massachusetts.

The most impressive change in city life was overhead, not underground. Thanks to cheap steel and the invention of a practical elevator, a ten-story building went up in Chicago in 1884. The Home Insurance Building became the nation's first skyscraper.

QUICK CHECK

Summarize **What new technologies changed city life in the late 1800s?**

EVENT

In 1871 most of Chicago's residents lived in wooden buildings. On October 8 fire swept through the city. Nearly a third of the city's people were left homeless. At least 250 died. By 1873 the city was entirely rebuilt.

The Great Chicago Fire

THE NEW AMERICANS

Except for Native Americans, the United States is a country of people who can trace their history to immigrants. Most immigrants came here between 1870 and 1924. During those years, more than 25 million immigrants entered the United States. They came on steamships, packed into crowded, bad-smelling quarters. Most came through Ellis Island in New York or Angel Island in San Francisco. During this time, most immigrants came from Southern and Eastern Europe. Many were Jewish or Catholic. Other immigrants came from China and Japan. Most arrived with little money, in search of new opportunities.

Hard Life in Cities

The majority of the immigrants settled where there were jobs—in cities of the Northeast. The streets of Boston, New York, Philadelphia, and later Chicago were filled with people speaking foreign languages.

Many new immigrants settled in **slums**—crowded neighborhoods with narrow, dirty streets. They were packed into rundown apartment buildings, called **tenements**. In the tenements, residents could get only very small amounts of fresh air and sunlight through tiny windows that looked out on the brick walls of neighboring buildings. Whole families often lived in a single room.

Despite new sewage systems, waste found its way into city drinking water. Diseases such as cholera and typhus spread quickly. A section of New York was called the "lung block" because so many people had tuberculosis.

Help for Immigrants

Many new immigrants were proud to be in the United States. Yet American life was harder than they had expected. Most immigrants struggled with the English language or didn't speak it at all. They had trouble communicating with landlords and employers. Many of them struggled to feel like Americans. One immigrant from Bulgaria wrote,

> "In Bulgaria I am not wholly a Bulgarian. In the United States I am not wholly an American."

Settlement Houses

In the late 1880s, Jane Addams, the daughter of a wealthy Illinois state senator, wanted to improve conditions in Chicago's slums. To do this, she felt she had to live among the people there. In 1889 Addams rented an old red-brick house surrounded by tenements. Educated women moved into the building. They helped homeless immigrants find housing. They taught English and job skills to adults. They opened kindergartens and music schools for

PEOPLE

Ida B. Wells was a well-known African American writer. In Memphis, Tennessee, she spoke out against violence toward African Americans. In Chicago, Wells worked with Jane Addams to prevent segregation in schools.

Ida B. Wells

▲ Jane Addams helped immigrants at Hull House in Chicago. Addams also fought for child labor laws.

children. Dances featured food and music from many different countries. Settlement houses worked to improve basic living conditions as well as promote education. Hull House became one of the first settlement houses in the United States. At settlement houses, workers did everything from making sure the city picked up garbage to inviting well-known speakers. The Chicago Tribune newspaper described the settlement houses as "A Project to Bring Rich and Poor Together."

By 1910 more than 400 settlement houses served immigrants in U.S. cities. Jane Addams went on to campaign for child labor laws, better housing, and world peace. In 1931 she won the Nobel Peace Prize.

▲ Families crowded together in tenements. Entire families sometimes lived in a single room.

QUICK CHECK

Summarize **How did Addams and other reformers help immigrants adjust to life in the United States?**

Americans have long been proud of their hospitality to immigrants. A famous poem carved into the base of the Statue of Liberty in New York City welcomes the world's "poor," its "homeless," and its "huddled masses." Yet by the early 1900s, many people felt it was time to close the door on immigration.

Many Americans blamed immigrants for the country's problems. Some American-born workers thought that immigrants would take away their jobs. Few of the new immigrants from Eastern and Southern Europe spoke English. As a result, they did not blend into American society as easily as some earlier immigrants. These fears led to restrictions on immigration to the United States.

◀ The Statue of Liberty

The Immigration Act of 1917 required immigrants to be able to read and write in some language. In 1924 Congress passed the Johnson-Reed Act. The new law placed tight limits on the number of immigrants allowed into the United States from certain countries or regions. The United States closed its doors to immigration. The immigration law was not changed for more than 40 years.

QUICK CHECK

Summarize How did immigration laws change after the arrival of immigrants from Eastern and Southern Europe?

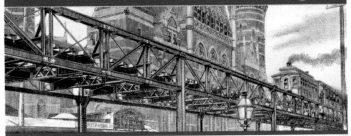

Check Understanding

1. **VOCABULARY** Imagine you are a new immigrant settling in Chicago in the late 1800s. Write a letter using these words.

   slum   tenement

2. **READING SKILL** Summarize Use the chart on page 306 to summarize the ways immigration changed American cities.

3. **Write About It** How did American industries help cities grow?

Map and Globe Skills
Use Cartograms

VOCABULARY

cartogram

Population can be shown on a map in different ways. One way is with a special kind of map called a **cartogram**. A cartogram shows information that can be measured in numbers. For example, to compare population numbers for different places, a cartogram changes the size of these places. You can compare populations by looking at the size of places.

Learn It

- Identify what is being shown in a cartogram. This cartogram shows the population of the U.S. in 1900.

- Read the map key to learn what each box represents. In 1900 how many people lived in Illinios?

- Ohio is larger than California on the cartogram. What does that tell you?

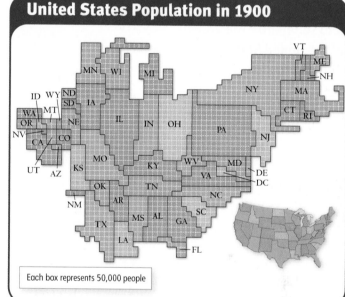

United States Population in 1900

Each box represents 50,000 people

Try It

- Which state on the cartogram had the largest population in 1900? Which state had the smallest population?

Apply It

- Draw a cartogram to compare the population of largest and smallest states in population today. Don't forget to include a legend and a title for your cartogram.

New States and Territories

Lesson 5

VOCABULARY

annex p. 313

Spanish-American War p. 314

buffalo soldier p. 315

READING SKILL

Summarize

Copy the chart below. Use it to summarize the growth of the United States in the late 1800s.

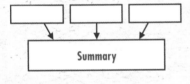

Summary

STANDARDS FOCUS

SOCIAL STUDIES Global Connections

GEOGRAPHY The World in Spatial Terms

In 1896 the discovery of gold in the Klondike region of Alaska drew thousands of people.

Visual Preview

Why did the United States gain power by 1900?

A The United States bought Alaska and took over Hawaii.

B In 1898 the United States defeated Spain in the Spanish-American War.

C Victory in the Spanish-American War made the United States a world power.

ALASKA AND HAWAII

By the 1890s, the borders of the United States stretched from the Atlantic Ocean to the Pacific Ocean and from Canada to Mexico. Eventually the land would be divided into 48 states. Some Americans wanted the United States to look for more land outside its borders.

The first places Americans turned their attention to were the huge, icy expanse of Alaska and the sunny islands of Hawaii.

Seward's Ice Box

In the 1860s Russia owned the vast wilderness of Alaska. It was home to the Inuit and some Russian fur traders. By 1867 the fur supply was nearly gone. Russia offered to sell the territory to the United States. Secretary of State William Seward agreed to pay $7.2 million for 500,000 square miles. That's an area one-fifth the size of the rest of the United States.

Many people disagreed with Seward's decision. They said Russian America, as it was called, was a large lump of ice, crowded with walruses. But Seward was determined. He insisted that the land contained vast natural resources. In 1896 prospectors proved him right. They found a huge field of gold in a region called the Klondike. Suddenly thousands of people rushed to make their home in "Seward's Icebox." Alaska became a state in 1959.

▲ Queen Liliuokalani

Hawaii Overthrown

In 1778 British explorer James Cook was the first European to land in Hawaii during his third voyage to the Pacific. On the island, he found a highly developed society. Cook was killed in a struggle there, but even after his death, Europeans remembered the beautiful islands.

Missionaries arrived in the 1820s to convert the islanders to Christianity. Immigrants from the United States discovered they could make a fortune growing sugarcane and pineapples. In 1893 American businessmen overthrew Hawaiian Queen Liliuokalani. Judge Sanford P. Dole became president of Hawaii the next year. In 1898 the United States wanted to build a naval base in the Pacific Ocean. Officials decided that Pearl Harbor in Hawaii was the best location, and Congress voted to **annex**, or take over, the islands. Hawaii became a state in 1959.

QUICK CHECK

Summarize **Why was Hawaii annexed?**

B PUSH FOR WAR

In 1898 Cuba and Puerto Rico were the only remaining Spanish colonies in the Americas. Cubans had been fighting for their independence since 1895. Many Americans wanted the United States to help the Cuban rebels. Newspaper owners William Randolph Hearst and Joseph Pulitzer tried to outdo each other with shocking reports of events in Cuba. This helped influence public opinion.

"Remember the *Maine*"

President William McKinley, who had fought in the Civil War as a young man, was not eager for war. He sent the U.S.S. *Maine* to Cuba to protect American citizens there.

On February 15, 1898, two explosions ripped through the *Maine*. The blast sunk the warship and killed 266 American sailors. No one ever discovered the cause of the explosion. Newspapers immediately blamed it on the Spanish. "THE WARSHIP MAINE WAS SPLIT IN TWO BY AN ENEMY'S SECRET. . . MACHINE," reported Hearst's *New York Journal*. Less than six weeks later, McKinley declared war on Spain.

The Rough Riders

The **Spanish-American War** became one of the shortest wars in American history. In May 1898 the U.S. Navy destroyed a

The World

MAINE EXPLOSION CAUSED BY BOMB OR TORPEDO?

Capt. Sigsbee and Consul-General Lee Are in Doubt---The World Has Sent a Special Tug, With Submarine Divers, to Havana to Find Out---Lee Asks for an Immediate Court of Inquiry---Capt. Sigsbee's Suspicions.

▼ A newspaper illustration showed the explosion of the U.S.S. *Maine*.

▲ Teddy Roosevelt led the Rough Riders against Spanish forces in Cuba.

Spanish fleet in the Philippine Islands, which were under Spanish control. In late June, American troops arrived in Cuba. They were poorly equipped and unorganized. Food supplies often spoiled on the way from Florida to Cuba. The cavalry had to leave its horses in Florida because there weren't enough boats to transport them. The heavy wool uniforms, many of which were left over from the Civil War, were too hot for the tropical climate.

Despite these problems, U.S. troops quickly overwhelmed the Spanish. Leading the fight was an energetic colonel named Teddy Roosevelt, who had been the secretary of the navy. When war broke out, he resigned to form a group of fighters called the Rough Riders. In Cuba, the Rough Riders led two important attacks, charging up Kettle Hill and San Juan Hill. They were joined by the **buffalo soldiers** of the 10th Cavalry. Buffalo soldiers were African American troops who had fought in the Plains Wars.

The war in the Caribbean was over in a matter of weeks. In the words of Secretary of State John Hay, the conflict between Spain and the United States was:

❝. . . a splendid little war.❞

QUICK CHECK

Summarize Why did American troops face difficulties in the first weeks of the Spanish-American War?

315

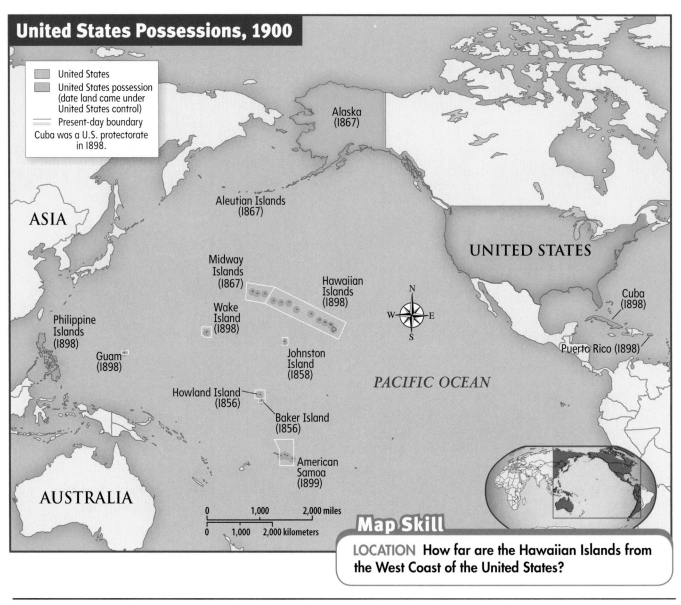

United States Possessions, 1900

Legend:
- United States
- United States possession (date land came under United States control)
- Present-day boundary

Cuba was a U.S. protectorate in 1898.

Alaska (1867)

ASIA

Aleutian Islands (1867)

UNITED STATES

Midway Islands (1867)

Hawaiian Islands (1898)

Cuba (1898)

Wake Island (1898)

Philippine Islands (1898)

Guam (1898)

Johnston Island (1858)

Puerto Rico (1898)

PACIFIC OCEAN

Howland Island (1856)

Baker Island (1856)

American Samoa (1899)

AUSTRALIA

0   1,000   2,000 miles
0   1,000   2,000 kilometers

Map Skill

LOCATION How far are the Hawaiian Islands from the West Coast of the United States?

Ⓒ AFTER THE WAR

In August 1898 the Spanish army decided to surrender. Spain gave up not only Cuba, but Puerto Rico and the island of Guam as well. Spain also sold the Phillipines to the United States for $20 million. The United States had fought to free Cuba. Now that the Americans had won the war, they faced difficult questions about what to do with new territories. Would the territories keep their independence? Would the Americans become colonial rulers like the Spanish?

In December of 1889, the Treaty of Paris answered these questions. The United States took a major step toward becoming a world power. Cuba won its independence, though the United States built a naval base on the island at Guantanamo Bay. Puerto Rico, Guam, and the Philippines became U.S. territories.

In the Philippines, rebels had been fighting the Spanish for years. They wanted to govern themselves, and they felt betrayed when the Americans took control of their island nation.

▲ U.S. soldiers were sent to the Philippines to fight rebels.

The rebels went to war again, this time against the new rulers. The war lasted for three years. More than 100,000 American soldiers were sent to the Philippines. Many of the American generals who led the troops had fought in the Plains Wars. More than 4,000 American soldiers died, mostly from disease.

Filipinos finally won their independence in 1946 after the end of World War II. Guam and Puerto Rico remain U.S. territories, and their people are American citizens.

QUICK CHECK

Summarize **Why did rebels in the Philippines fight American soldiers?**

Check Understanding

1. **VOCABULARY** Write one sentence using two of the three terms below.

   annex   buffalo soldier
   Spanish-American War

2. **READING SKILL** Summarize What was the result of the Spanish-American War?

3. **Write About It** How did the United States acquire Alaska, Hawaii, and other territories between 1867 and 1898?

Unit 7 Review and Assess

Vocabulary

Number a paper from 1 to 4. Beside each number, write the word that matches the description.

exoduster   reservation

settlement house   monopoly

1. An area of land put aside for Native Americans

2. African American who moved to Kansas in the 1860s

3. A business that completely controls an industry

4. A community center that provides services to the poor

Comprehension and Critical Thinking

5. How did the Homestead Act encourage people to settle on the Great Plains?

6. **Reading Skill** Why did the United States drive the Lakota from the Black Hills?

7. **Critical Thinking** Why did the Central Pacific Railroad take longer to build than the Union Pacific?

8. **Critical Thinking** Why did many people dislike monopolies?

Skill

Use Cartograms

Compare the cartogram on page 311 with the cartogram on the right. Answer each question with a complete sentence.

10. In which map is California larger? Why?

11. Which state had the largest population in 1850?

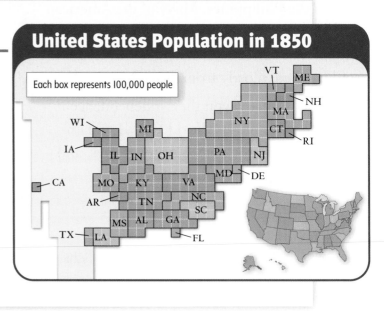

United States Population in 1850

Each box represents 100,000 people

Test Preparation

Use the bar graph below to answer the questions.

Immigration to the United States, 1907

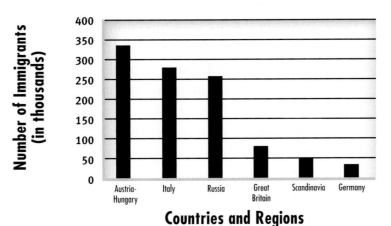

Countries and Regions

1. Where did the most immigrants come from in 1907?

   A. Russia

   B. Austria-Hungary

   C. Italy

   D. Germany

2. About 30,000 immigrants came to the United States from Japan in 1907. Where would Japan appear on the bar graph?

   A. Between Great Britain and Scandinavia

   B. After Germany

   C. Before Austria-Hungary

   D. Between Italy and Russia

3. What information can be determined from reading the graph?

   A. The three countries or regions from which the most immigrants came

   B. The religion of the immigrants who arrived

   C. The regions where immigrants settled

   D. The number of immigrants from France

4. About how many immigrants in all are shown on the graph?

5. Write one sentence explaining what the graph tells you.

How does technology change people's lives?

Write About the Big Idea

Expository Essay
Use the Unit 7 Foldable to help you write an expository essay that answers the Big Idea question, *How does technology change people's lives?* Be sure to begin your essay with an introduction. Add a paragraph for each invention on your Foldable. End with a concluding paragraph that summarizes the effects of the inventions.

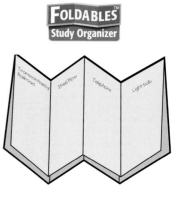

FOLDABLES™
Study Organizer

Diary of a Cattle Drive

It's 1880 and you're on a cattle drive from north Texas to Abilene, Kansas. Here's what you need to know to write a diary of the cattle drive.

1. You will cover a distance of more than 1,000 miles. Cattle can travel about 10 miles a day, so you'll be on the trail for four months.

2. You will spend 10 to 12 hours a day in the saddle, in all kinds of weather.

3. At night, by the light of a campfire, you take your diary from your saddlebags.

Write at least three diary entries about the cattle drive.

My Diary

Tuesday. A bad thunderstorm today scared the herd. We chased cattle for miles. I'm cold and wet tonight. Even a campfire can't warm me.

Friday. We're thirty miles outside of Abilene. I'm dusty and tired. With luck, I'll be riding back to Texas next week with money in my saddlebags.

Unit 8

Essential Question
How does a nation protect its freedom?

FOLDABLES™
Study Organizer

Make Inferences
Make and label a Concept Map Foldable book before you read this unit. Across the top write **How to protect freedom**. Label the three tabs **Danger**, **Action**, and **Result**. Use the foldable to organize information as you read.

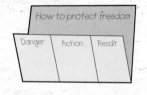

How to protect freedom

| Danger | Action | Result |

LOG ON
Find out more about Unit 8 at
www.macmillanmh.com

THE MODERN ERA

PEOPLE, PLACES, AND EVENTS

Theodore Roosevelt

Rosa Parks

Panama Canal

Montgomery, Alabama

1906
Theodore Roosevelt visits Panama during the construction of the canal.

1955
Rosa Parks refuses to give up her seat on a public bus.

1900

1925

1950

In 1906 **President Theodore Roosevelt** visited Panama, making him the first President to leave the country while in office.

Today more than 10,000 ships pass through the **Panama Canal** each year.

In 1955 **Rosa Parks** was arrested when she refused to give her bus seat to a white man.

Today you can visit the Rosa Parks Library and Museum in **Montgomery, Alabama.**

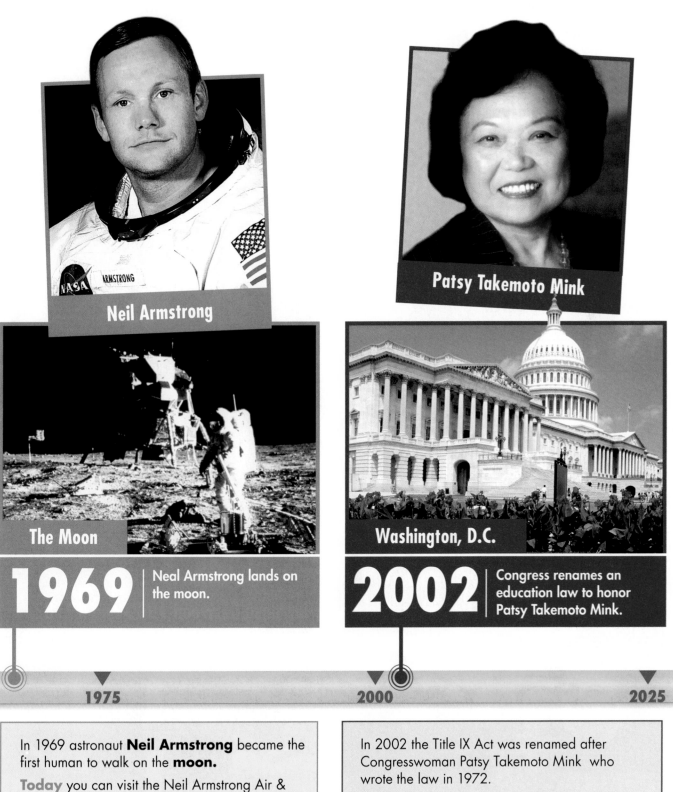

Neil Armstrong

Patsy Takemoto Mink

The Moon

Washington, D.C.

1969
Neal Armstrong lands on the moon.

2002
Congress renames an education law to honor Patsy Takemoto Mink.

1975

2000

2025

In 1969 astronaut **Neil Armstrong** became the first human to walk on the **moon.**

Today you can visit the Neil Armstrong Air & Space Museum in Wapakoneta, Ohio.

In 2002 the Title IX Act was renamed after Congresswoman Patsy Takemoto Mink who wrote the law in 1972.

Today a portrait of **Patsy Takemoto Mink** hangs in the Capitol in **Washington, D.C.**

323

A New Century

VOCABULARY

progressive p. 325

reform p. 325

muckraker p. 325

Treaty of Versailles p. 330

League of Nations p. 330

READING SKILL

Make Inferences

Copy the chart below. Use it to make inferences about Theodore Roosevelt.

Text Clues	What You Know	Inference

STANDARDS FOCUS

| SOCIAL STUDIES | Science, Technology, and Society |
| GEOGRAPHY | Environment and Society |

Theodore Roosevelt giving a campaign speech

Visual Preview

How did United States power increase between 1900 and 1918?

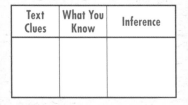

A Progressives pushed for more government control on American business.

B The Panama Canal made travel between the Atlantic and Pacific Oceans easier.

C The United States entered World War I when Germany sank U.S. ships.

D The U.S. Senate refused President Wilson's request to join the League of Nations.

A ROOSEVELT'S SQUARE DEAL

On September 6, 1901, President William McKinley was shot at a fair in Buffalo, New York. He died eight days later. Vice President Theodore Roosevelt became President at age 42.

Theodore Roosevelt returned home from the Spanish-American War a hero. By the time he became President, industry had made some Americans rich. But millions of Americans worked long hours in dangerous conditions for low wages.

Some people complained about the gap between the rich and the poor. They called themselves **progressives** because they believed in social progress. They looked to President Roosevelt as a progressive leader. He said people needed fair treatment—"a square deal":

> **"**This country will not be a . . . good place for any of us to live in unless we make it a . . . good place for all of us to live in.**"**

Business Changes

Roosevelt pushed for **reforms** in business and government. Reforms are changes designed to improve the lives of many people. Many people, however, believed that government should leave businesses alone. Journalists called **muckrakers** attacked this idea. Muckrakers were writers who dug up dirt, or "muck," about dangerous working conditions and dishonest politicians.

In 1903 muckraker Ida Tarbell wrote about John D. Rockefeller's Standard Oil Company. She accused Rockefeller of forming a trust—a combination of businesses that work to get rid of competition. Soon after Tarbell's articles appeared, Congress broke Standard Oil into several smaller companies.

Ida Tarbell

National Parks

President Roosevelt loved the outdoors. He pushed for laws that would protect, or conserve, America's natural resources. Roosevelt created 5 national parks and set aside 51 wildlife refuges.

QUICK CHECK

Make Inferences Why did people consider Theodore Roosevelt a progressive?

Yellowstone National Park

President Roosevelt could never resist a challenge. In 1902 he approved one of the biggest construction projects ever attempted. Over the next 12 years, thousands of workers would carve out 240 million cubic yards of earth to separate North America and South America. The result was the Panama Canal.

Central American Shortcut

When the European explorers arrived in the Americas, they searched eagerly for the Northwest Passage, a water passage from the Atlantic to the Pacific Ocean. None was ever found. Ships had to travel around the southern tip of South America to reach the Pacific Ocean. By the end of the Spanish-American War, American businesses needed a cheaper, easier way to ship products between the two oceans. The U.S. Navy needed a quicker path to conflicts around the world. A canal across Panama would cut the trip from the Atlantic Ocean to the Pacific Ocean by 7,000 miles. France began building a canal in 1880. The project failed. Twenty years later, the United States offered to complete the canal.

Construction of the canal took more than eight years. Many people came to Panama from the West Indies to work on it. The money they earned allowed them to move with their families to the United States.

In 1900 Panama was a province of Colombia. Colombia wanted more money than President Roosevelt was willing to spend for the right to build the canal. In 1903 he sent the Navy to help Panama gain independence from Colombia. The United States then bought a ten-mile-wide strip of land across Panama. It was called the Canal Zone.

Building the Canal

Before work on the canal could begin, the Canal Zone had to be made safe for workers. Malaria and yellow fever killed thousands of people there every year. Doctors had recently learned that mosquitoes spread those diseases quickly from person to person. An Army doctor named William Gorgas came up with a solution. He instructed workers to drain swamps, spread oil and insecticide over standing water, and cut the grassy areas where the mosquitoes laid their eggs. By 1906 yellow fever had been eliminated and the number of malaria cases was greatly reduced. Finally, in August 1914, the first ship made the first 48-mile voyage through the canal from the Atlantic Ocean to the Pacific Ocean.

QUICK CHECK

Make Inferences How did oil help in the construction of the Panama Canal?

About 14,000 ships cross the Panama Canal each year. Some large, modern ships, such as aircraft carriers, are too large to use the canal. ▼

ⓒ WORLD WAR I

In 1914 Archduke Francis Ferdinand of Austria-Hungary was assassinated in the country of Serbia. At that time, most European countries belonged to one of two alliances. On one side were the Allied Powers—Great Britain, France, and Russia. On the other side were the Central Powers—Germany, Turkey, and Austria-Hungary. After the assassination of the archduke, Austria-Hungary declared war on Serbia, an ally of Russia. Soon other nations entered the war. World War I had begun. The United States did not enter the war until 1917.

Deadly Modern Weapons

World War I introduced new weapons such as poison gas, machine guns, and tanks. German submarines, called U-boats, sank merchant ships. In 1917 Germany declared all-out submarine warfare on Allied ships. For the first time, airplanes were used to bomb targets.

◀ The United States entered World War I in 1917. A newspaper printed this headline after Congress voted to declare war.

▼ American soldiers spent months in muddy trenches.

As fighting in Europe continued, each side built ditches, called trenches, that extended for miles along the battlefront. The zone between these ditches was called "no man's land." This type of fighting became known as trench warfare. Thousands of soldiers on each side were killed or wounded trying to gain a few acres of land. Thousands more died from diseases caused by living in dirty conditions in the trenches for months at a time.

Meanwhile, the war at sea continued. In 1915 the Germans sank the *Lusitania*, a British passenger ship with 128 Americans on board. This act enraged Americans.

The United States Enters the War

In early 1917 the Germans sank eight American ships. In April President Woodrow Wilson asked Congress to declare war on the Central Powers. This raised the spirits of the Allies. U.S. warships began to protect merchant ships crossing the Atlantic Ocean. American soldiers did not reach Europe until early 1918. By the time American troops arrived in Europe, the Central Powers, led by Germany, were near defeat. They had lost many men and were running low on food, ammunition, and other resources. Hundreds of thousands of soldiers had been killed.

African American soldiers fought in key battles that helped the Allies gain the advantage. Over 300,000 African Americans joined the army and navy. However, they were assigned to segregated units.

The Home Front

The nation's industries had to expand to meet the needs for supplies and weapons during the war. Millions of men had left their jobs to serve in the military. This provided job opportunities for women and minorities.

During the war the United States had to produce enough food for those at home and the Allied forces. Americans helped in any way they could. They cut back on eating such things as meat and sugar so there would be enough for the soldiers.

A World War I poster

QUICK CHECK

Make Inferences What made World War I different from other wars you have read about in this book?

Ⓓ MAKING PEACE

World War I ended on November 11, 1918. It claimed the lives of 8.5 million soldiers. Later a peace treaty, the **Treaty of Versailles**, was signed. It treated Germany harshly. The Allied powers who signed the treaty blamed Germany for starting the war. Germany was forced to pay the costs of fighting the war.

President Wilson wanted World War I to be "the war to end all wars." To prevent future wars, he proposed an organization in which nations could solve their problems peacefully. He called this organization the **League of Nations**. The U.S. Senate, however, refused to approve the League. Some Senators feared that the United States might be drawn into the political problems of countries far from U.S. borders. The United States, one of the most powerful nations in the world, did not join the League of Nations. This later would be one factor that caused the organization to fail.

QUICK CHECK

Make Inferences **Why would Germans feel bitter about being blamed for starting the war?**

Check Understanding

1. **VOCABULARY** Write a paragraph describing one of President Theodore Roosevelt's accomplishments. Use the following vocabulary words in your writing.

progressive   reform

muckraker

Text Clues	What You Know	Inference

2. **READING SKILL** Make Inferences Use your chart from page 324 to write about why the U.S. Senate did not approve the entry of the United States into the League of Nations.

3. **Write About It** Why did the United States decide to enter Word War I?

▼ Woodrow Wilson giving a campaign speech

Map and Globe Skills

Use Time Zone Maps

VOCABULARY

time zone

In 1878 Sanford Fleming of Canada suggested dividing the world along the lines of longitude into 24 equal **time zones**— areas that have the same time throughout. After railroads were built, times zones were introduced because of confusion over train schedules. Study the map below.

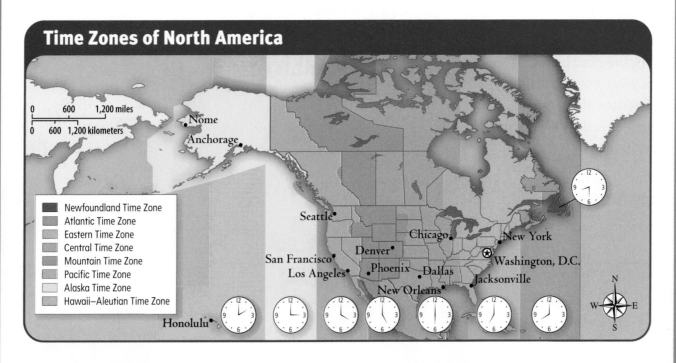

Time Zones of North America

0   600   1,200 miles
0   600 1,200 kilometers

- Newfoundland Time Zone
- Atlantic Time Zone
- Eastern Time Zone
- Central Time Zone
- Mountain Time Zone
- Pacific Time Zone
- Alaska Time Zone
- Hawaii–Aleutian Time Zone

Nome
Anchorage
Seattle
Chicago
New York
San Francisco
Denver
Washington, D.C.
Los Angeles
Phoenix
Dallas
Jacksonville
New Orleans
Honolulu

Learn It

- Each stripe represents one time zone.

- Sometimes the time zones follow national or state borders.

- The time for each zone is shown at the bottom of the map when it is noon at the Prime Meridian.

- As you go west or to the left, one hour is subtracted for each time zone. As you go east to the right, one hour is added.

Try It

- If it is noon in Denver, what time is it in Washington, D.C.?

Apply It

- Suppose you traveled from Los Angeles to Honolulu by plane. When you arrive how would you have to change your watch?

GOOD TIMES, HARD TIMES

VOCABULARY

suffrage p. 333

mass production p. 335

assembly line p. 335

stock p. 337

READING SKILL

Make Inferences

Copy the chart below. As you read, use it to make inferences about the changes in daily life during the 1920s.

Text Clues	What You Know	Inference

STANDARDS FOCUS

SOCIAL STUDIES Production, Distribution, and Society

GEOGRAPHY Human Systems

SIGNATURES OF N.Y. STATE WOMEN WANT THE V

VOTES FOR WOMEN A SUCCE

VOTE Y

After many years of protests, women finally won the right to vote in 1920.

Visual Preview

How did economic and political changes affect American freedoms?

A Women won the right to vote and many African Americans moved to cities.

B Mass production offered Americans new products that were sold by advertising.

C People feared discrimination, and the United States economy crashed.

D The New Deal used government programs to fight the Great Depression.

A AN IMPORTANT DECADE

During the "Roaring Twenties," day-to-day life changed more quickly than ever before. Many people could afford exciting new products, like cars. All of this spending caused big problems by the end of the decade.

The 1920s were a time of social change. Two of the most important changes during those years involved women and African Americans.

Women's Right to Vote

Since the early 1800s, American women had been fighting for **suffrage**, or the right to vote. Over the years, women such as Susan B. Anthony and Carrie Chapman Catt had carried on the fight. The first state to grant women's suffrage was Wyoming in 1869. But a Constitutional amendment did not come until 51 years later. After women's contributions during World War I, American lawmakers finally voted for women's suffrage. In 1920 the Nineteenth Amendment gave women the right to vote.

The Great Migration

During the first decades of the twentieth century, more than one million African Americans left the South. They wanted to escape racial violence and the Jim Crow laws that took away their voting rights. A boll weevil infestation of cotton crops ruined the harvest causing loss of jobs for field workers. Many African Americans moved to cities in the North and the Midwest. There they found jobs in steel mills and automobile plants. They often faced discrimination there as well, but life there was generally safer and they were able to find jobs. This movement of African Americans from the South is called the Great Migration. During the Great Migration, Chicago's African American population doubled, Cleveland's tripled, and Detroit's became six times larger.

QUICK CHECK

Make Inferences Why did women have to fight for the right to vote?

EVENT

In the 1920s, many African Americans settled in the Harlem section of New York City. Harlem became a center for black artists such as painter William Johnson, poet Langston Hughes, and jazz musician Duke Ellington. They were part of the **Harlem Renaissance**.

Harlem Renaissance

Several important changes took place in the 1920s that affected the daily lives of most Americans. Many items we use every day were introduced during this time. Because life changed rapidly in exciting ways, the decade became known as the Roaring Twenties.

Automobiles Change America

During the 1920s, the automobile, once a costly luxury, became affordable to millions of families. This brought about many other changes in American society and the economy.

The increasing number of cars created a need for highways, gas stations, motels, and roadside diners. The oil industry grew rapidly because of the need for gasoline and motor oil.

The greatest luxury of today!
AIR-COOLED MOTORING in the World's Fastest Road Car.... *now at new, low prices!*

FRANKLIN

THE ONE-THIRTY SEDAN $2180   THE ONE-THIRTY-FIVE SEDAN $2485   THE ONE-THIRTY-SEVEN SEDAN $2775

▲ Assembly line workers build cars. On an assembly line, each worker does one job over and over.

Advertising in newspapers and magazines reached millions of Americans.

Listening to the radio became part of American family life. Millions of American homes had these new devices.

To meet the demand for cars, a system known as **mass production** was used. Mass production means making a large number of products quickly. Automaker Henry Ford used an **assembly line** to mass produce his cars. On an assembly line, a product is built as it moves past workers. Each person does one job, such as tightening a bolt. By 1925 one Ford came off the assembly line every 10 to 15 seconds.

Age of Wonders

Modern household goods such as vacuum cleaners, electric stoves, and refrigerators were also mass produced in the 1920s. Some homes had these new devices. Entertainment also changed, and new ways of reaching a wide audience were developed. These new media included the radio and movies. Most American homes had radios. People went to the movies in their free time.

Buying on Time

Magazine and radio advertisements persuaded people to buy new items. Many people who could not afford the items bought on credit. Consumers borrowed money to pay for goods, then paid it back over time. Some people, however, were unable to pay back the money they had borrowed. That would lead to economic problems by the end of the 1920s.

QUICK CHECK

Make Inferences **How did new media help business leaders like Henry Ford?**

335

▲ Assembly lines made more products than people could buy.

▲ The stock market collapse hurt the American economy.

ⓒ HARD TIMES

The 1920s were exciting for many Americans. However, some of the worst discrimination in our nation's history occurred during this time.

Immigration Limits

Widespread prejudice toward immigrants from Eastern and Southern Europe arose in the 1920s. This anti-immigrant attitude led Congress to pass laws limiting immigration. In 1924 the National Origins Act ended almost all immigration to the U.S. for 40 years.

Ku Klux Klan

The prejudice toward immigrants led to a revival of the Ku Klux Klan. The Klan had threatened newly freed African Americans, but had been inactive since the late 1800s. In

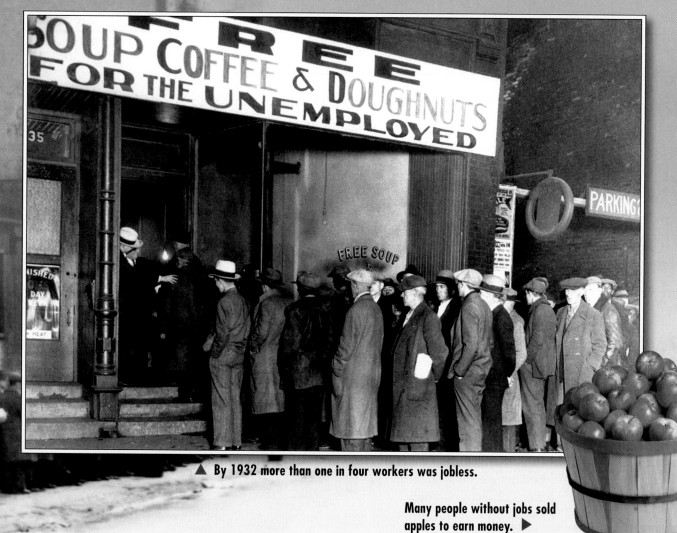

▲ By 1932 more than one in four workers was jobless.

Many people without jobs sold apples to earn money. ▶

the 1920s, membership grew to more than 4 million. The Klan expanded the groups it targeted to include Jews, Catholics, and immigrants from Southern Europe.

The Economy Crashes

By late 1929 the U.S. economy faced serious problems. Mass production had led to more goods than people needed. Also, many people were still paying for items they had purchased on credit.

When people stopped buying, companies could not make profits. Many companies were owned by stockholders. A **stock** is a share in the ownership of a company. People buy and sell stocks on the stock market, an organized system for buying and selling shares. Many people had also borrowed money to buy stocks.

During this time profits were falling. Many stockholders decided to sell, but there were few buyers. Many stocks suddenly became almost worthless. People who had borrowed money to buy stocks could not repay their debts. On Tuesday, October 29, 1929, the stock market crashed. This event began a period known as the Great Depression, a period of severe economic hardship in the 1930s.

QUICK CHECK

Make Inferences **How did mass production hurt businesses in the late 1920s?**

A TIME OF CRISIS

The stock market crash forced many banks to close. Companies went out of business. Even worse, unemployment skyrocketed. More than one in four workers became jobless. Many people lost their homes. Some people were forced to live in shacks and tents that were called "Hoovervilles" after the President in 1929, Herbert Hoover.

By 1932 the nation faced the worst economic crisis in its history. Franklin D. Roosevelt won the presidency that year by promising Americans a "New Deal." He said he would use the power of the U.S. government to put people to work.

Government Steps In

In Roosevelt's first 100 days in office, Congress passed many laws that set up new agencies. They were called "alphabet" agencies due to their initials. Government

New Deal Programs	
Civilian Conservation Corps (CCC)	put people to work planting trees and fighting forest fires
Agricultural Adjustment Act (AAA)	helped farmers get higher prices for their crops
Federal Deposit Insurance Corporation (FDIC)	insured banks and protected people's money
Tennessee Valley Authority (TVA)	brought electricity to rural areas of Tennessee and bordering states

▼ The Hoover Dam was built across the Colorado River.

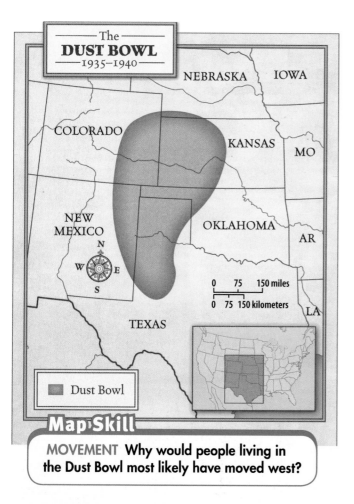

The
DUST BOWL
— 1935–1940 —

NEBRASKA   IOWA

COLORADO   KANSAS   MO

NEW MEXICO   OKLAHOMA   AR

N W E S

0   75   150 miles
0   75   150 kilometers

TEXAS   LA

◼ Dust Bowl

Map Skill

MOVEMENT Why would people living in the Dust Bowl most likely have moved west?

programs hired workers to build dams in the West. These included the Hoover Dam on the Colorado River and the Grand Coulee Dam on the Columbia River.

Drought Destroys Farmland

The nation's economy was also hurt by a natural disaster. For several years beginning in 1930, a severe drought dried out Midwestern farmlands. High winds blew away millions of acres of soil. This area came to be known as the Dust Bowl. Many farm families were forced to leave their land to seek jobs on the West Coast.

Women Play Key Roles

President Franklin Roosevelt had an important ally in his wife, Eleanor Roosevelt. She traveled the country and reported

conditions to him. Frances Perkins, the first woman to serve in a President's cabinet, also helped support the New Deal. As the Secretary of Labor, she fought to get Congress to pass two programs that are widely known today. One was Social Security, designed to help people after they retire. The other was unemployment insurance, which paid money for a certain period of time to people who were jobless.

QUICK CHECK

Make Inferences **How did the drought in the 1930s hurt farm families?**

Check Understanding

1. **VOCABULARY** Write a paragraph about the American economy in the 1920s using the vocabulary words from below.

   mass production   assembly line   stock

2. **READING SKILL Make Inferences** Use the chart from page 332 to explain how the government helped people in the Great Depression.

Text Clues	What You Know	Inference

 EXPLORE The Big Idea

3. **Write About It** Write an essay about whether the 1924 immigration law protected or hurt our freedoms.

Lesson 3

VOCABULARY

dictator p. 341

neutral p. 341

ration p. 342

internment p. 343

concentration camp p. 345

READING SKILL

Make Inferences

Copy the chart below. Use it to make inferences about the changes World War II caused at home.

Text Clues	What You Know	Inference

STANDARDS FOCUS

 SOCIAL STUDIES Global Connections

GEOGRAPHY Human Systems

WORLD WAR II

The Japanese attack on Pearl Harbor brought the United States into World War II.

Visual Preview

How did World War II affect the United States?

A The United States entered World War II after the Japanese attacked Pearl Harbor.

B Americans helped at home, but Japanese Americans were forced into camps.

C The war ended in 1945 with the defeat of Germany and the surrender of Japan.

Ⓐ WORLD WAR AGAIN

*By the end of the 1930s, the world was at the edge of war.
Germany, Italy, and Japan threatened world peace.
These nations called themselves the Axis Powers.
Standing against them were the Allied Powers of Europe.*

By the early 1930s, Adolf Hitler was the leader of Germany. Hitler was a **dictator**, or absolute ruler. His followers were called Nazis. On September 1, 1939, the Nazi army invaded Poland. In response, Great Britain and France, the Allied Powers, declared war on Germany. This was the beginning of World War II.

At the start of the war, it looked as if the Axis Powers, which included Germany, Italy, and Japan, would win easily. By 1940 France had fallen. Led by Winston Churchill, Great Britain was able to hold off German attempts to invade. In June 1941, Hitler attacked the Soviet Union, which was ruled by dictator Josef Stalin.

As in World War I, the United States tried to remain **neutral**, or not take sides. Most Americans supported the Allies, but they did not want to go to war. That feeling was about to change.

Attack on Pearl Harbor

By 1941 Japan had conquered much of China. Japan began to take control of resource-rich areas across the Pacific Ocean. In response, the United States restricted trade with Japan. It also tried to force Japan to withdraw from China. Instead Japanese leaders made plans to attack the United States.

On December 7, 1941, Japan launched a surprise attack on Pearl Harbor, a United States naval base in Hawaii. The next day, Congress declared war on Japan. Three days later, Nazi Germany and Italy declared war on the United States.

QUICK CHECK

Make Inferences **Why did Japan attack Pearl Harbor?**

Adolf Hitler, the leader of the Nazis, ruled Germany from 1933 until 1945. ▶

341

Deaths in World War II

(Bar graph showing Deaths in Millions by Country: Soviet Union ~13, China ~3.5, Germany ~3.5, Japan ~1.7, United States ~0.4)

▲ United States air power was critical to victories against Japan on islands in the Pacific Ocean.

B WAR ON TWO FRONTS

For the first time, the United States had to fight on two fronts, or areas of battle. Americans fought in the Pacific Ocean and Asia. They also fought in Europe and Africa.

Six months after Pearl Harbor, American planes and warships sunk several Japanese aircraft carriers in a battle at Midway Island in the Pacific. It was an important victory. The U.S. Navy and Marines had to fight across many other Pacific islands for three more years to reach islands near Japan.

Trouble for the Axis

Meanwhile, the Allies fought in Europe and Africa against Italy and Germany. By the middle of 1943, German forces had been driven out of the Soviet Union and North Africa. In addition, American, British, and Canadian troops had invaded Italy, which surrendered on September 3. The Allies then made plans to invade France.

War at Home

While armed forces were fighting, American industries turned out war supplies. Millions of women joined the workforce. In 1943 nearly 40 percent of all factory workers were women. Minorities also filled jobs that had been closed to them in the past. By 1943 U.S. factories were making two bombers to every German bomber.

Americans at home worked together to help win the war. Across the United States items such as sugar, meat, and gasoline were **rationed**, or limited. Ration coupons allowed a family to buy only a certain amount of some items.

Changing Roles

For the first time, women also joined the army and the navy. As many as 150,000 women joined the Women's Army Corps (WAC).

An additional 27,000 women joined the WAVES, or "Women Accepted for Volunteer Emergency Service" to serve in the U.S. Navy.

African Americans served in all branches of the military. One African American unit, the Tuskegee Airmen, became famous fighter pilots. A Hispanic marine, Guy Gabaldon, won a Silver Star for capturing 1,000 Japanese soldiers on the island of Saipan.

Japanese Americans in Camps

After Pearl Harbor some people feared that Japanese Americans were secretly allied with Japan. In February 1942, President Roosevelt ordered for over 100,000 Japanese Americans to be taken from their homes to live in **internment** camps. People lost their freedom, homes, businesses, and possessions. Located mostly in desert areas, these camps isolated Japanese Americans in crowded and uncomfortable conditions. The final camp wasn't closed until March 1946.

QUICK CHECK

Make inferences Why were Japanese Americans sent to internment camps?

Japanese Americans were forced to live in internment camps far from their homes during World War II. ▼

Citizenship

Working for the Common Good

To keep food on the table during World War II, Americans planted victory gardens. They grew food in backyards, in empty lots, and even on city rooftops. You can work for the common good in your community by volunteering at a senior citizen center or a community garden. Or you can help people who have lost their homes in natural disasters. Another way to work for the common good is to clean up parks in your neighborhood.

Write About It Make a plan for a project at your school that would help everyone. List jobs for students in each grade.

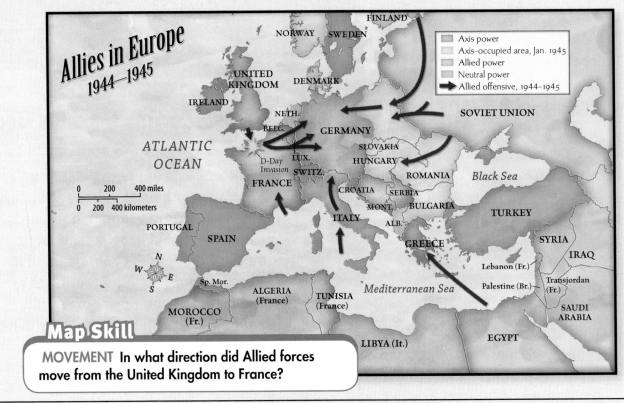

Allies in Europe 1944–1945

Legend:
- Axis power
- Axis-occupied area, Jan. 1945
- Allied power
- Neutral power
- → Allied offensive, 1944–1945

FINLAND, NORWAY, SWEDEN, UNITED KINGDOM, DENMARK, IRELAND, NETH., BELG., GERMANY, SOVIET UNION, ATLANTIC OCEAN, D-Day Invasion, LUX., SWITZ., FRANCE, SLOVAKIA, HUNGARY, ROMANIA, Black Sea, CROATIA, SERBIA, MONT., BULGARIA, TURKEY, ALB., PORTUGAL, SPAIN, ITALY, GREECE, SYRIA, IRAQ, Lebanon (Fr.), Transjordan (Fr.), Palestine (Br.), Sp. Mor., ALGERIA (France), TUNISIA (France), Mediterranean Sea, SAUDI ARABIA, MOROCCO (Fr.), LIBYA (It.), EGYPT

0 200 400 miles
0 200 400 kilometers

N W E S

Map Skill

MOVEMENT In what direction did Allied forces move from the United Kingdom to France?

C   THE WAR ENDS

D-Day Landing

On June 6, 1944, the Allies landed at Normandy on the coast of France. This was D-Day, which means the day an operation starts. The bloody battle killed thousands of soldiers on the beaches. Despite many deaths, the Allies were victorious. They pushed the Germans away from the coast. D-Day marked the beginning of the end for Germany.

Allied soldiers came ashore at Normandy in France on D-Day. ▶

Allied forces had Germany surrounded on three sides. The Soviets came in from the east. The British and Americans attacked from the south through Italy and the west across France.

On April 30, 1945, as Allied forces approached Germany's capital, Hitler committed suicide. Hitler's rule had lasted 12 years. Germany surrendered on May 7, ending the war in Europe.

The Holocaust

Hitler often spoke out against Jewish people. As the Nazi party gained power in Europe, it targeted Jewish people and other groups. Jews and other Europeans were taken from their homes and held in **concentration camps.** This became known as the Holocaust. In the camps, many were worked to death as slave laborers. Many others were killed by Nazi soldiers. Those who did not die were mistreated. About 10 million people died during the Holocaust, including 6 million Jewish people.

Atomic Weapons

On the Pacific front in 1945, it appeared that the United States would have to invade Japan to win the war. Instead a new weapon, the atomic bomb, was used against Japan.

On August 6, 1945, the United States dropped a single atomic bomb on the city of Hiroshima, Japan. This bomb killed about 75,000 people. A few days later, a second bomb was dropped on Nagasaki. Japan surrendered on August 14, 1945.

QUICK CHECK

Make Inferences **How did Americans at home help win World War II?**

American soldiers freed prisoners from concentration camps. ▶

Check Understanding

1. **VOCABULARY** Write four sentences to summarize events from this lesson using the vocabulary terms.

dictator	ration
neutral	internment

2. **READING SKILL** Make Inferences. Use the chart from page 340 to write about how World War II changed life in the U.S.

Text Clues	What You Know	Inference

3. EXPLORE The Big Idea **Write About It** Write an essay explaining how the United States protected its freedoms after being attacked at Pearl Harbor.

345

Lesson 4

VOCABULARY

communism p. 347

truce p. 349

arms race p. 349

satellite p. 351

era p. 351

READING SKILL

Make Inferences

Copy the chart below. As you read, use it to make inferences about the Cold War.

Text Clues	What You Know	Inference

STANDARDS FOCUS

| SOCIAL STUDIES | Power, Authority, and Governance |
| GEOGRAPHY | Places and Regions |

THE COLD WAR

An atomic bomb test in the 1950s in Nevada

Visual Preview

How did world changes affect the United States from 1945 to 1960?

A NATO and the United Nations formed to prevent wars and fight communism.

B Communism, the Korean War, and an arms race made the 1950s a tense time.

C A space race and crises over Berlin and Cuba worried Americans.

A NEW WORLD POWER

At the end of 1945, the United States was the most powerful nation in the world. But tensions grew between the United States and the Soviet Union, two nations that had been allies during World War II.

Many Americans disliked Josef Stalin, the dictator of the Soviet Union. Millions of his own people died as a result of his cruelty. The Soviet Union took control of much of Eastern Europe in the years following World War II. It forced these countries to follow its economic system, called **communism**. In this system, the government owns all property and resources. Americans believed that if communism spread, it would destroy the United States. This distrust led to the Cold War. This struggle was called "cold" because the United States and the Soviet Union never attacked each other. Instead they fought with ideas, money, and words.

The Effects of World War II

In 1945, as World War II ended, many nations joined together to form the United Nations, or UN. World leaders hoped that it could solve problems peacefully and improve the lives of all people.

A number of nations—including the United States, Great Britain and France—also joined together in 1949 to create the North Atlantic Treaty Organization, or NATO. The nations agreed to fight the spread of communism. The Soviet Union responded by forming an alliance with countries in Eastern Europe called the Warsaw Pact.

President Harry Truman then sponsored the Marshall Plan. This plan provided $13 billion in food and goods to help Western Europe recover from the damage caused by the war. It also helped prevent the spread of communism.

QUICK CHECK

Making Inferences Why did the United States and the Soviet Union become enemies after World War II?

Josef Stalin, leader of the Soviet Union ▶

A battle during
the Korean War

B COMMUNISM SPREADS

By the beginning of 1946, the Soviet Union controlled many countries in Eastern Europe. Among them was the eastern half of Germany and half of its capital, Berlin. Berlin is located entirely within East Germany. The spread of communism worried British leader Winston Churchill, who said in a speech that "an Iron Curtain" had descended across Europe. "Behind the Iron Curtain" was a phrase used to describe countries under Communist control.

A New Threat

In 1949 the Soviet Union successfully tested an atomic bomb. After this event, people worried that a war between the Soviet Union and the United States might become an atomic war that could cause the end of the world.

The Korean War

At the end of World War II, American and Soviet troops entered Korea to disarm the Japanese troops stationed there. The allies divided Korea at the 38th parallel of latitude. American troops controlled the south, while Soviet troops controlled the north. In 1950 war broke out on the Korean peninsula, which was divided into two countries, North Korea and South Korea.

As the Cold War began, talks to unify Korea broke down. South Korea became a republic and North Korea had a communist government. In June 1950, North Korea invaded South Korea. Troops from the United States and 16 other countries in the United Nations fought together to drive them back. A new war had begun.

The North Koreans, helped by Chinese Communist troops, used Soviet weapons, including fighter jets. Thousands of American and UN soldiers were killed. In addition, millions of Korean civilians were killed or driven from their homes.

The Korean War ended in 1953 when a **truce** was signed. A truce is an agreement to stop fighting. This truce left the border between North and South Korea where it had been in 1950.

A Time of Tension

During the 1950s, the United States and the Soviet Union continued to develop more powerful atomic weapons called nuclear weapons. This buildup is called the **arms race**. Some American families, fearful of war, built bomb shelters in their homes. Fear of a nuclear attack was part of daily life. Both the United States and the Soviet Union spent enormous amounts of money on weapons.

QUICK CHECK

Make Inferences **Why did the Soviets and the United States take opposite sides in the Korean War?**

◀ During the arms race, U.S. missiles were built to carry nuclear weapons called warheads.

Americans sometimes call the 1950s "The Eisenhower Years." Dwight D. Eisenhower served as President from 1953 to 1961. Enormous changes in American life occurred during these years. People had more money to spend than ever before. Many Americans bought products such as televisions and cars. Others bought houses in the growing areas outside of cities, called suburbs.

McCarthyism Uses Fear

Some lawmakers used the fear of communism to gain power. In 1950 Senator Joseph McCarthy accused many Americans of being Communists. Some people who were accused lost their jobs. The senator's unfair attacks became known as McCarthyism. In 1954 Congress publicly reprimanded McCarthy for his actions.

The Berlin Wall

Between 1949 and 1962, about 2.5 million East Germans escaped to West Germany through West Berlin. For example, one day the entire math department of a university left the country. East Germany needed educated workers for its economy.

In 1961 the leader of the Soviet Union, Nikita Khrushchev, ordered a wall built to separate communist East Germany from West Berlin and East Berlin. This wall prevented East Germans from escaping. The Berlin Wall

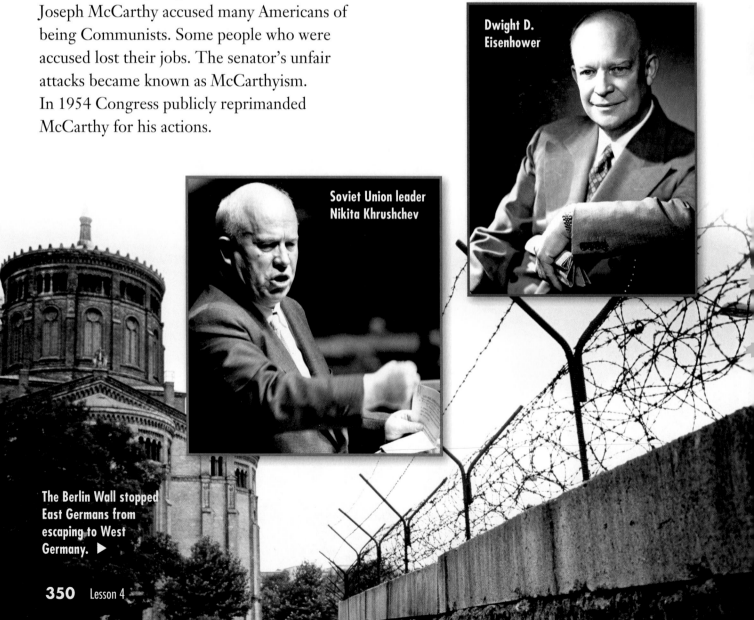

Dwight D. Eisenhower

Soviet Union leader Nikita Khrushchev

The Berlin Wall stopped East Germans from escaping to West Germany. ▶

Neil Armstrong took this picture of astronaut Edwin "Buzz" Aldrin, the second man to walk on the moon. ▶

became a symbol of the divisions between communism and democracy.

The Space Race

In 1957 the Soviets launched a **satellite**, called *Sputnik*, into orbit around Earth. A satellite is an object that circles another object. The United States then created its own space program. The two countries raced to get farther into space. On July 20, 1969, American Neil Armstrong became the first human being to walk on the moon. Armstrong said:

❝That's one small step for a man, one giant leap for mankind.❞

Cuban Missile Crisis

For many people, the most frightening event of the Cold War **era**—or period of history— was the Cuban Missile Crisis. In 1959 Fidel Castro led a successful revolution in Cuba, an island nation that is just 90 miles from Florida. After the revolution, Cuba became the first communist nation in the Americas.

In 1962 Khrushchev placed nuclear missiles in Cuba. President John F. Kennedy ordered a naval blockade of Cuba to keep Soviet ships from bringing more missiles to Cuba. Many Americans feared an attack would be launched from Cuba. After tense talks, Khrushchev ordered Soviet ships to turn back. Soviet missiles in Cuba were taken apart. In return, the United States promised not to attack.

QUICK CHECK

Make Inferences **How was the space race part of the Cold War?**

Check Understanding

1. **VOCABULARY** Write four sentences to summarize the Cold War using these vocabulary terms.

   communism   satellite
   arms race   era

2. **READING SKILL** Make Inferences Use your chart from page 346 to help you write about the Cold War.

Text Clues	What You Know	Inference

3. **Write About It** Write an essay describing President Kennedy's response to threats from the Soviet Union.

VOCABULARY

Civil Rights Act p. 354

prejudice p. 354

Voting Rights Act p. 355

migrant farm worker p. 356

READING SKILL

Make Inferences

Copy the chart below. As you read, use it to make an inference about how the civil rights movement changed the United States.

Text Clues	What You Know	Inference

STANDARDS FOCUS

SOCIAL STUDIES Individuals, Groups, and Institutions

GEOGRAPHY Human Systems

A TIME OF CHANGE

The March on Washington took place on August 28, 1963.

Visual Preview

How did issues of equality affect the United States?

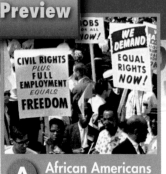
A African Americans fought against segregation in schools and other public places.

B Two major laws granted people civil rights and voting rights.

C Many groups, including women, sought and received more rights.

D The last 30 years saw war in Vietnam, scandals, and close elections.

Ⓐ SEPARATE BUT NOT EQUAL

After World War II, news of the Holocaust shocked people throughout the world. As a result, many Americans began to question discrimination that was happening in the United States.

In 1896 the U.S. Supreme Court ruled in *Plessy* v. *Ferguson* that separate but equal conditions were constitutional. This allowed racial segregation of schools. Schools remained separate, but not equal. In 1909 the National Association for the Advancement of Colored People, or NAACP, was founded to fight discrimination and segregation.

Segregation Becomes Illegal

NAACP lawyer Thurgood Marshall took on several cases of people who wanted to end school segregation. The issue made it to the Supreme Court with *Brown* v. *Board of Education*. On May 17, 1954, the Supreme Court overturned *Plessy* v. *Ferguson*, and school segregation became illegal.

The Montgomery Bus Boycott

The fight against segregation spread. On December 1, 1955, Rosa Parks, an African American, boarded a bus in Montgomery, Alabama. She sat in a seat in the back of the bus reserved for African Americans. As the bus filled, the driver changed the whites only section to include Parks's seat. He ordered Parks to give up her seat. That was the law.

Parks refused and was arrested. In protest, the NAACP organized a bus boycott. For nearly a year, protesters drove to work in carpools or walked. Finally, in November 1956, the Supreme Court ruled that bus segregation was illegal.

In 1960 African American college students staged "sit-ins" at lunch counters for "whites only." They refused to leave until they were served or arrested. Court cases followed. As a result, restaurants in 126 American cities were desegregated.

QUICK CHECK

Make Inferences **Why did courts decide that segregation was wrong?**

Thurgood Marshall was a U.S. Supreme Court Justice from 1967 to 1991. ▶

Dr. Martin Luther King, Jr., a Baptist minister, was one of the organizers of the Montgomery bus boycott. By 1963 this civil rights leader organized many protests against segregation, including protests in Birmingham, Alabama, one of the most segregated cities in the United States.

March on Washington

In August 1963, King and other civil rights leaders led 250,000 people in the March on Washington. They demanded job opportunities and a civil rights law. King gave a speech that spoke of his "dream" for a world free of prejudice. Read part of his speech on this page.

The March on Washington was a great moment for the civil rights movement. Soon afterward, President John F. Kennedy asked Congress to pass a federal civil rights bill. He did not live to see the bill become law. On November 22, 1963, the President was in Dallas, Texas. He was riding in a convertible so the crowd could see him. Shots were fired and hit Kennedy. Although the car sped to the hospital, the President was dead.

The Civil Rights Act

After Kennedy's assassination, Vice President Lyndon B. Johnson became President. He worked to pass the **Civil Rights Act** of 1964. The law made it illegal for employers to discriminate, or show **prejudice**, against someone because of race, color, religion, nationality, or gender. Prejudice is a negative opinion formed without proof.

Primary Sources

I have a dream that one day this nation will rise up and live out the true meaning of its **creed**: "We hold these truths to be self-evident, that all men are created equal . . . ."

I have a dream that my four little children will one day live in a nation where they will not be judged by the color of their skin but by the content of their character . . . .

This will be the day when all of God's children will be able to sing with a new meaning, "My country, 'tis of thee, sweet land of liberty, of thee I sing. Land where my fathers died, land of the pilgrim's pride, from every mountainside, let freedom ring."

A section from the "I have a dream" speech by Martin Luther King, Jr., August 28, 1963, Washington, D.C.

creed   stated belief

Write About It Write a speech about a dream that you have for the future.

Even with the Civil Rights Act, unfair and illegal practices, such as charging taxes at voting places, still existed in the South. This led Congress to pass the **Voting Rights Act** of 1965. This law allowed federal agents to use their power to make sure all citizens were allowed to vote.

The War on Poverty

In 1964 more than one in five Americans lived in poverty. To solve this problem, President Johnson declared a "war on poverty." Johnson wanted to build what he called "The Great Society" that provided health care and education to all Americans. One program that was passed then was Medicare. It helps people over age 65 pay for medical care.

By the middle of the 1960s, the civil rights movement had registered thousands of voters. Lunch counters, schools, and other public places had been integrated. Conditions for many African Americans, however, had not improved. More than half lived in poverty. In 1968 King launched a "Poor People's Campaign" to call attention to poverty among African Americans. There were people who thought that King's nonviolent approach was no longer useful. Some African Americans listened to another leader, named Malcolm X. At first, Malcolm X said

PEOPLE

Like her husband, Dr. Martin Luther King, Jr., **Coretta Scott King** fought segregation. She also worked for equal rights for all women. The Coretta Scott King Award is given each year for outstanding children's books.

Coretta Scott King

that working with whites would not achieve equal rights for African Americans. By 1964, however, Malcolm X believed that people of all races could work together for change.

Violence took the lives of both Malcolm X and Martin Luther King, Jr. An assassin killed Malcom X in the spring of 1965. On April 4, 1968, Martin Luther King, Jr., was in the city of Memphis, Tennessee, to support a strike. Shots rang out, and King was assassinated.

QUICK CHECK

Make Inferences How can helping people pay for medical care benefit society?

President Kennedy (far right) is shown speaking in 1962. Lyndon Johnson (right) was sworn in as President immediately after Kennedy's death. Jacqueline Kennedy, the President's widow, stood to Johnson's left. ▶

After 1960 more groups sought equal rights. Protests were organized for improved working conditions and equal pay.

Helping Migrant Workers

One group that protested during the 1960s was **migrant farm workers**. Migrant farm workers travel from farm to farm to harvest crops. These workers faced dirty and dangerous working conditions for little pay. In 1962 two Mexican Americans, César Chávez and Dolores Huerta, organized a labor union that later became the United Farm Workers, or UFW. The union led strikes and boycotts against farm owners. In time, the efforts of the UFW brought higher wages and better working conditions to migrant workers.

The Women's Movement

Women gained the right to vote in 1920, but many women still said that they did not have economic equality. In 1960 women were paid less than men for doing the same jobs. In 1966 writer Betty Friedan formed the National Organization for Women (NOW). NOW insisted that the government enforce the Civil Rights Act of 1964, which made it illegal to discriminate against women in the workplace.

In 1972 Congresswoman Patsy Mink wrote a law giving women equal rights in education. This law, first known as Title IX, expanded women's sports programs in schools. In 2002 the law was renamed in honor of Patsy Takemoto Mink.

César Chávez (right) urged workers to strike (huelga) for better wages and workers' rights.

From left to right, Betty Friedan, Margaret Heckler, Barbara Mikuski, and Bella Abzug marching for women's rights in Washington, D. C.

Rights for Native Americans

In 1968 a group organized the American Indian Movement (AIM) which worked for equal rights and the improvement of living conditions. It also drew attention to poverty on reservations. After many protests, the Supreme Court ruled that states had to honor treaty agreements. As a result, millions of acres were returned to Native Americans in Alaska, Maine, New Mexico, and South Dakota during the 1970s.

People with Disabilities

For years, millions of Americans with disabilities faced discrimination at work, education, housing, and transportation. In 1990 the Americans with Disabilities Act, or ADA, made it illegal to discriminate against people who are disabled. It also required the removal of barriers that prevent disabled people from gaining access to public facilities.

QUICK CHECK

Make Inferences **How did Title IX help women's sports programs to grow?**

AIM members protest anti-Indian legislation in Washington, D.C.

President George H. W. Bush signs the Americans with Disabilities Act in 1990.

1974

Watergate Scandal

In 1974 evidence showed that President Richard M. Nixon used his power to prevent an FBI investigation into spying on his political opponents. To avoid impeachment, or formal charges of misconduct, Nixon became the first President to resign, or quit, the office of President.

1979

Iran Hostage Crisis

Revolutionaries stormed the U.S. embassy in Tehran, Iran, and took American hostages. They demanded the return of their former leader to stand trial. The 14-month crisis ended when the United States and Iran signed the Algiers Accords, and the 52 hostages were released.

1985

U.S.-Soviet Arms Talks

President Ronald Reagan and Soviet leader Mikhail Gorbachev met in 1985 to discuss a reduction of nuclear weapons. Two years later, an arms treaty was signed. It called for the United States and the Soviet Union to destroy their nuclear missiles.

D THE VIETNAM WAR

More than 10,000 miles from the fight for equal rights in the United States, a bloody fight was raging—the Vietnam War. This war divided many Americans. North Vietnam was a communist nation supported by the Soviet Union and China. South Vietnam was a republic backed by the United States. The United States worried that if Vietnam became entirely communist, other Asian countries would fall to communism.

The War Begins

In August 1964, President Johnson announced that North Vietnamese torpedo boats had fired on two American warships in the Gulf of Tonkin. What Johnson did not say was that the American warships were helping South Vietnam to spy and conduct raids on North Vietnam. After the North Vietnamese attacked a military base in South Vietnam, killing 7 Americans and wounding 100, President Johnson responded. Less than 14 hours after the attack, some 132 American aircraft bombed North Vietnam. By the end of 1966, 450,000 American troops were fighting an all-out war there.

Protesting the War

Americans became deeply divided over the war. People called "Hawks" believed the United States had to fight North Vietnam to stop communism from spreading. Those called "Doves" believed that the United States should not fight in a war where its own safety was

1989

Cold War Ends

In November 1989, protests forced the East German government to open the border between East and West Germany. The protesters destroyed the Berlin Wall. One by one, communist governments across Eastern Europe also fell. In 1991 the Soviet Union broke up into 15 independent countries.

1998

Presidential Impeachment

Bill Clinton of Arkansas was elected President in 1992. He had successes both at home and overseas, including strengthening the economy and working for peace. In his second term, Clinton was accused of lying under oath. He was impeached by the House. The Senate voted to let him stay in office.

2000

Close Election

The 2000 election between Al Gore and George W. Bush was a close race. Bush had a slim lead in Florida. But the race was so close that a recount was required by law. Five weeks later, the Supreme Court ruled there wasn't time for a recount. Gore accepted the decision, and Bush won the election.

not threatened. In 1969 more than 250,000 protesters came to Washington, D.C., to speak out against the war. Soon, President Richard M. Nixon withdrew some troops, but the war continued.

In 1973 U. S. troops stopped fighting in Vietnam, but they continued to help South Vietnamese troops. In 1975 North Vietnam won the war, and Vietnam was united under a communist government. In the two decades of fighting, nearly two million Vietnamese people were killed. More than 57,000 Americans died in the war.

QUICK CHECK

Make Inferences **Why did doves protest against the Vietnam War?**

Check Understanding

1. **VOCABULARY** Write about how protests affected the following laws.

   Civil Rights Act   Voting Rights Act

2. **READING SKILL** Make Inferences Use your chart from page 352 to help you write about the civil rights movement.

Text Clues	What You Know	Inference

3. **Write About It** Write about the basic freedoms for which protesters and activists were fighting.

359

Present-day Challenges

VOCABULARY

terrorism p. 361

interdependence p. 364

North American Free Trade Agreement p. 364

global warming p. 364

READING SKILL

Make Inferences
Use the chart below to make an inference about why the United States is fighting a war on terrorism.

Text Clues	What You Know	Inference

STANDARDS FOCUS

SOCIAL STUDIES	People, Places, and Environments
GEOGRAPHY	Human Systems

A fiery blast rocked the World Trade Center. Its two towers in New York City were hit by jet airliners on September 11, 2001.

Visual Preview

What challenges does the United States face in the 21st century?

A The war on terrorism began after the September 11, 2001, attacks.

B U.S. soldiers are fighting a war on terrorism in Afghanistan and Iraq.

C Global warming is one of the challenges we face in the future.

A SEPTEMBER 11, 2001

On September 11, 2001, men armed with box cutters hijacked four jet airliners. Two airliners were flown into the World Trade Center in New York City. One hit the Pentagon in Washington, D.C. The fourth crashed in a field in Pennsylvania. Over 3,000 people died in the attacks.

The men who hijacked the planes on September 11, 2001, committed acts of **terrorism**. Terrorism is the use of fear and violence by non-government groups against civilians to achieve political goals.

Terrorism in the United States

There have been many acts of terrorism in American history. Since World War II, many terrorist attacks on Americans have been carried out by Muslim groups from the Middle East. A Muslim is someone who follows the religion of Islam. A few radical Muslims who want their society to be very strict are willing to use violence to force change. They think European and American ideas have hurt their society. They also think Israel should not exist.

The attacks of September 11, 2001, were carried out by a terrorist group called Al Qaeda. Al Qaeda was created in 1988 by Osama bin Laden, a wealthy Saudi Arabian, to aid Muslims fighting Soviet troops in Afghanistan. The Soviet Union had invaded Afghanistan in 1979. After the Soviets retreated in 1989, Al Qaeda wanted to drive all Europeans and Americans out of Muslim nations, destroy Israel and unite all Muslims under a strict form of Islam. Al Qaeda began attacking Americans in the Middle East and Africa in the 1990s.

President Bush was careful to explain that Islam was not to blame for the September 11, 2001 attacks. He said:

> The enemy is not our many Muslim friends. . . .
> Our enemy is a radical network of terrorists. . . .
>
> —GEORGE W. BUSH

QUICK CHECK

Making Inferences **What were the results of al Qaeda's use of terrorism?**

361

WAR ON TERRORISM

President Bush told Afghanistan to turn over Osama bin Laden and other members of Al Qaeda to the United States. Afghanistan was ruled by a radical group called the Taliban that supported Al Qaeda. They refused the President's demands. The United States and its allies then invaded Afghanistan. They drove the Taliban from power and helped the people elect a new government. Osama bin Laden escaped and the Taliban's forces fled to the mountains to continue the fight. President Bush said the war would not end until:

"every terrorist group of global reach has been found, stopped, and defeated."

The Invasion of Iraq

President Bush worried that terrorists might obtain weapons of mass destruction. Weapons of mass destruction can kill many people all at once. A nuclear bomb is one example of a weapon of mass destruction.

One country that concerned the President was Iraq. It had tried to build nuclear weapons and had helped terrorists. Iraq was led by a dictator named Saddam Hussein. In 1990 it invaded the country of Kuwait to seize Kuwait's oil. The United States and its allies drove the Iraqis out of Kuwait, but the war made Iraq an enemy of the United States. The American Government became concerned that Iraq might help terrorists attack the U.S.

▲ U. S. and Iraqi soldiers fighting militia insurgents in Iraq

▲ Iraqi voters' ink-stained fingers became a badge of honor.

The United States and a coalition of allies were convinced that Iraq was hiding weapons of mass destruction. In 2003 they invaded Iraq. Saddam Hussein was captured. United States and coalition forces helped the Iraqi people hold free elections for the first time. No weapons of mass destruction were found.

Former members of Saddam Hussein's forces continued to fight, and Al Qaeda sent people to Iraq as well. At the same time, Iraqi society divided into several groups. Each formed a militia, and they began to fight with each other and against American troops. By mid-2007, the war in Iraq continued and over 3000 U.S. soldiers had been killed.

QUICK CHECK

Make Inferences. **Why did many Americans turn against the Iraq War in 2006?**

363

The economies of the world's countries are connected. Trade allows countries to export goods and raw materials. It also allows them to import goods and materials they need. This **interdependence**, or dependence on each other to meet needs and wants, allows countries to specialize in certain products and materials.

Trade agreements help countries do business. The **North American Free Trade Agreement**, or NAFTA, is one example. In 1993 Canada, Mexico, and the United States agreed to eliminate trade barriers among the three countries. This formed one of the largest free-trade zones in the world. Since then, the United States has increased the amount of goods it ships to Canada and Mexico.

Environmental Issues

As the global economy grows, it can improve the lives of millions of people. The growing economy can also affect the environment. Most factories, automobiles, and power plants burn fossil fuels—coal, oil, or natural gas. This releases pollution into the air that mixes with water vapor and falls as acid rain. Acid rain negatively affects the quality of soil and surface water in some areas of the United States.

Pollution has created another serious problem, **global warming**. Global warming is an overall rise in Earth's temperature. Burning fossil fuels release gases, especially carbon dioxide, into the atmosphere. Many scientists believe these gasses help trap the sun's heat near earth, causing a rise in temperature. This trapping of heat is called the greenhouse effect.

The rise in temperatures from global warming may contribute to extreme weather conditions, including powerful hurricanes. In 2005 a record number of hurricanes hit the United States. The worst hurricane, Katrina, flooded New Orleans, Louisiana, and the coast of Mississippi. More than 1,000 people died. Thousands of people lost their homes and everything they owned.

Hurricane Katrina survivors are rescued from a rooftop.

Solar panels, such as these on the space station, may one day send energy back to Earth.

The Future

The biggest changes in your lifetime may result from developments in science and technology. The science of genetics is one example. Scientists use computers to map the genes in the human body. Genes are tiny parts of cells that determine how you look and grow. Doctors hope to use genetic research to cure diseases and help people live longer.

Scientists are also trying to change the way we produce energy. Oil and coal supplies are likely to run out. Before they do, we need more clean and renewable sources of energy. These include sun, wind, and fuels such as ethanol, which is made from corn. Countries such as Denmark produce large amounts of energy with huge windmills. Someday, we may even place huge panels in space to collect solar energy and send it back to Earth.

QUICK CHECK

Make Inferences **What prediction can you make about the ways technology will benefit people in the future?**

Check Understanding

1. **VOCABULARY** Write about the global economy. Use these vocabulary terms.

   interdependence
   North American Free Trade Agreement

2. **READING SKILL** Make Inferences Use your chart from page 360 to write about the war on terrorism.

Text Clues	What You Know	Inference

3. **Write About It** Write about how the United States has tried to protect its freedoms since the attacks of September 11, 2001.

Vocabulary Review

Number a paper from 1 to 4. Beside each number write the word from the list below that matches the description.

muckraker   stock

suffrage   truce

1. A share in the ownership of a company

2. An agreement to end fighting, but not a war

3. A writer who dug up dirt about big business

4. The right to vote

Comprehension and Critical Thinking

5. What factors led to the Great Depression?

6. **Reading Skill** How did the Cold War affect the lives of Americans?

7. **Critical Thinking** Why were thousands of Japanese Americans placed in internment camps?

8. **Critical Thinking** What effect did the civil rights movement have on the people of the United States?

Skill

Use Time Zone Maps

Write a complete sentence to answer each question.

9. Is the time earlier or later in the time zones west of where you live?

10. If you live in Honolulu and need to call a friend in Alaska at 10 A.M., at what time should you make the call from your home?

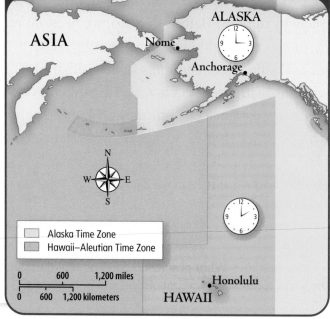

Alaska and Hawaii Time Zones

ASIA

ALASKA

Nome

Anchorage

N
W — E
S

☐ Alaska Time Zone
☐ Hawaii–Aleutian Time Zone

0   600   1,200 miles
0   600   1,200 kilometers

Honolulu

HAWAII

Test Preparation

Study the bar graph. Then answer the questions.

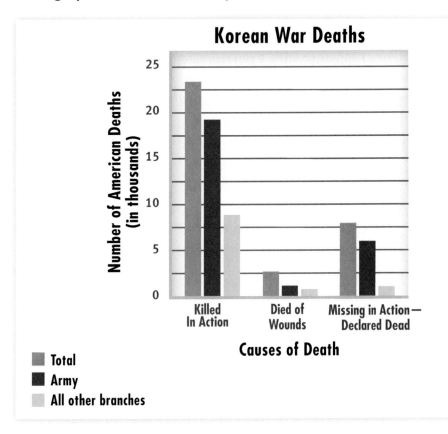

Korean War Deaths

Number of American Deaths (in thousands)

Causes of Death

Killed In Action • Died of Wounds • Missing in Action—Declared Dead

■ Total
■ Army
▢ All other branches

1. What amount does each horizontal line on the bar graph represent?

A. 5,000

B. 500

C. 2,500

D. 25,000

2. About how many Americans were killed in action during the Korean War?

A. 1,900

B. 19,000

C. 2,300

D. 23,000

3. What other ways might be used to show this data?

A. Map

B. Venn diagram

C. Climograph

D. Line graph

4. What does this bar graph tell you about the U. S. Army during the Korean War?

5. What does this bar graph tell you about the soldiers missing in action during the Korean War?

How does a nation protect its freedom?

Write About the Big Idea

A Persuasive Essay

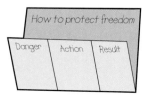

How to protect freedom

Danger	Action	Result

Use the Unit 8 Foldable to help you write a persuasive essay that answers the Big Idea question, *How does a nation protect its freedom?* Begin with a paragraph that gives an example of a time when our nation's freedom was in danger. Explain the action taken and the result of that action. Conclude with an inference about why it is important to protect our nation's freedom.

Create a Newspaper Article

Work in small groups to create a front page news story about an event that you have read about in Unit 8. There are several parts to an article. Follow these steps to create your own front page story.

1. Decide who should write the article.

2. Then one person should find and cut out or copy photographs and illustrations for the page.

3. Another person should find and make a copy of a map or chart that helps to explain the story.

As a group, decide how you want your page to look. Then choose a headline for your article.

GLOBAL WARMING
Polar Bears' Habitat Melting

Global warming is a threat to the survival of polar bears. The World Conservation Union has estimated that the polar bear population will drop by 30 percent over the next 45 years. In Canada, numbers fell by 22 percent between 1997 and 2004.

Reference Section

The Reference Section is a collection of tools that can be used to help you understand the information you read in this textbook.

Draw Conclusions

Reading for understanding is more than noticing the details in a passage. Readers need to think about what the details tell them. Often the details in a passage will help you draw a conclusion. Drawing a conclusion is reaching an opinion based on the details you read.

Learn It

- Gather details and other evidence in a reading passage.

- Identify the subject of the passage.

- Look for connections between the pieces of information. Ask yourself what the evidence says about the subject.

- Draw a conclusion based on what you have read.

- Read the passage below and think about what conclusions you can draw from it.

Text clue   The British march into the nation's capital.

Text clue: Dolley Madison had finished preparations for a dinner party.

Text clue   British troops reached the White House.

Text clue   The British ate a meal before burning the White House.

The War of 1812

On the evening of August 24, 1814, British troops marched into Washington, D.C. After setting fire to the Capitol building, they marched down Pennsylvania Avenue toward the White House. First lady Dolley Madison had just finished preparations for a dinner for forty people when she heard the British cannons. She grabbed several paintings and fled the White House as the British arrived. After eating a meal, the British set fire to the White House.

Try It

Copy and complete the graphic organizer below. Fill in lines on the left with the text clues. Fill in the box on the right with a conclusion based on the evidence you gathered.

Text Clues	Conclusion

What conclusion did you draw about where the British ate dinner?

Apply It

● Review the steps for drawing conclusions in Learn It.

● Read the paragraph below. Then use a graphic organizer to draw a conclusion about where Francis Scott Key was when he watched the battle of Fort McHenry.

The British attack on Fort McHenry began September 13. For 25 hours, the fort was bombarded by more than 1,500 cannonballs and rockets. Francis Scott Key, an American prisoner on a British ship, watched the night sky light up with "the rockets' red glare." The next morning, Key saw that the American flag still flew over Fort McHenry. Key expressed his feelings in "The Star-Spangled Banner," a poem that later became our national anthem.

Unit 6 • Reading Skills

Fact and Opinion

When people write about events, they often include both facts and opinions. Facts are statements that can be proven true. Opinions state feelings and beliefs. Opinions cannot be proven true or false. Being able to distinguish facts from opinions will help you understand what you read in social studies.

Learn It

- Facts can be checked and proven true.

- Opinions are personal views. They cannot be proven true or false.

- Clue words such as *think, felt, believe,* and *it seems* often state opinions.

- Now read the passage below. Look for facts and opinions.

The Underground Railroad

In 1849 Harriet Tubman heard that she and other enslaved workers on her Maryland plantation were to be sold farther south. Tubman believed that life there would be more difficult. She fled from the plantation in the middle of the night. After traveling 90 miles, she reached the free soil of Pennsylvania. She later said, "I felt like I was in heaven."

Fact
After traveling 90 miles, she reached the free soil of Pennsylvania.

Opinion
I felt like I was in heaven.

Try It

Copy and complete the chart below. Fill in the chart with two facts and two opinions from the paragraph about the Underground Railroad on page R12.

Fact	Opinion

How did you figure out which phrases were facts and which were opinions?

Apply It

- Review the steps for understanding fact and opinion from Learn It.

- Read the paragraph below. Then make a chart that lists two facts and opinions from the paragraph.

Ulysses S. Grant was Lincoln's best general and he seemed fearless. Lincoln decided to put Grant in charge of the entire Union army. He hoped Grant would bring the ugly war to an end.

Grant had two major goals. First, he planned to destroy Lee's army in Virginia. After that, he planned to capture Richmond, the capital of the Confederacy.

For 40 days, from April to June 1864, Grant battled Lee again and again across Virginia. Finally, Grant surrounded Lee in Petersburg, and put the city under siege. In the end, Grant captured Richmond. But he wasted the lives of thousands of Union troops. The Confederacy would have fallen without Grant's attacks.

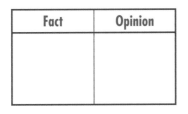

Summarize

Summarizing is a good way to remember what you read. After you read a paragraph or section in your textbook, make a summary of it. A summary is a brief statement about the topic of a passage. Since a summary leaves out minor details, it should be short.

Learn It

- Find key details that tell more about a subject.
- Leave out details that are not important.
- Restate the important points briefly in a summary.
- Read the passage below and think about how you would summarize it.

Topic The Buffalo	

THE BUFFALO

Key detail
Buffalo were important to Native Americans of the Plains.

Key detail
Settlers and railroad workers almost killed off buffalo.

Unimportant detail
Fewer than 1,000 buffalo were left in 1900.

Native Americans hunted buffalo on the Great Plains for centuries. These large animals were the most important part of Native American life on the Great Plains. They provided food, shelter, tools, and clothing.

Before settlers and railroads arrived, around 50 million buffalo roamed the Great Plains. Over a period of about 40 years, settlers and railroad workers slaughtered most of the huge animals. By 1900 fewer than 1,000 buffalo were left.

Copy and complete the summary chart below. Fill in the top box with pieces of information from the passage on page R14. Add one important detail of your own. Then write a summary based on the information you gathered.

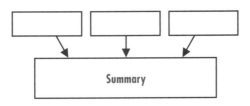

Summary

What is the difference between a summary and a main idea?

● Review the steps for summarizing in Learn It.

● Read the paragraphs below. Then summarize the passage using a summary chart.

In 1868 the United States signed a treaty with the Lakota, granting them large areas of land, including the Black Hills area of present-day South Dakota. The Black Hills had deep religious meaning to the Lakota. But in 1874 Americans discovered gold in the Black Hills. Immediately thousands of miners set off into this sacred part of the Lakota territory.

The Lakota chiefs, including Sitting Bull and Crazy Horse, refused to allow miners to dig in the Black Hills. As a result, U.S. soldiers arrived to drive Sitting Bull and the other chiefs onto reservations away from the area.

Make Inferences

When you read information, sometimes meanings or connections are not clear. That's when it's important to make inferences about the text. An inference is something you figure out based on clues and information that you already know. Making inferences gives a better understanding of what you read. It also helps you make sense of new information.

Learn It

- Identify details and clues in the text.

- Combine the clues with your own experience and what you know.

- Make an inference that tells more about what happened.

- Read the passage below. Think about inferences you can make about what happened.

Rockefeller and Tarbell

Text clue
Tarbell accused Rockefeller of forming a trust.

Text clue
In 1911 Standard Oil was broken into smaller companies.

In 1903 Ida Tarbell wrote about John D. Rockefeller's Standard Oil Company. She accused Rockefeller of forming a trust. A trust is a combination of businesses whose owners cooperate to get rid of competition. Tarbell wasn't the first person to criticize trusts. In 1890 Congress had passed the Sherman Antitrust Act to control big business. But the law was rarely enforced. Soon after Tarbell's articles appeared, President Theodore Roosevelt put the Sherman Act to use. In 1911 Standard Oil was broken into smaller companies.

Try It

Copy the chart below. In the first column, list text clues from the passage on page 1. In the second column, add what you know. In the third column, make an inference about how Standard Oil was broken into smaller companies.

Text Clues	What You Know	Inference

What inference can you make about Rocekfeller's feelings toward Tarbell?

Apply It

- Review the steps to make inferences in Learn It.

- Read the selection below. Using statements from the passage, create a chart that makes an inference about how cars changed the American economy in the 1920s.

During the 1920s, the automobile, which was once a costly luxury, became affordable to millions of families. Assembly lines turned out millions of cars to meet the demand. As more families bought cars, people needed places to take cars for gasoline and engine repair. Cars became the main form of public transportation. Suddenly there was a need for highways, service stations, and roadside restaurants.

Geography Handbook

Geography and You

Many people think geography means learning about the location of cities, states, and countries, but geography is much more than that. Geography is the study of our Earth and all its people. Geography includes learning about bodies of water such as oceans, lakes, and rivers. Geography helps us learn about landforms such as plains and mountains. Geography also helps us learn about using land and water wisely.

People are an important part of the study of geography. Geography includes the study of how people adapt to live in new places. How people move, how they transport goods, and how ideas travel from place to place are also parts of geography.

In fact, geography has so many parts that geographers have divided the information into smaller groups to help people understand its ideas. These groups are called the six elements of geography.

Six Elements of Geography

The World in Spatial Terms: Where is a place located, and what land or water features does that place have?

Places and Regions: What is special about a place, and what makes it different from other places?

Physical Systems: What has shaped the land and climate of a place, and how does this affect the plants, animals, and people there?

Human Systems: How do people, ideas, and goods move from place to place?

Environment and Society: How have people changed the land and water of a place, and how have land and water affected the people who live in a place?

Uses of Geography: How has geography influenced events in the past, and how will it influence events now and in the future?

Five Themes of Geography

You have read about the six elements of geography. The five themes of geography are another way of dividing the ideas of geography. The themes, or topics, are **location**, **place**, **region**, **movement**, and **human interaction**. Using these five themes is another way to understand events you read about in this book.

1. Location

The White House

In geography, *location* means an exact spot on the planet. A location is usually a street name and number. You write a location when you address a letter.

2. Place

The Grand Canyon

A *place* is described by its physical features, such as rivers, mountains, or valleys. Human features, such as cities, language, and traditions can also describe a place.

3. Region

Wheat field in the Midwest

A *region* is larger than a place or location. The people in a region are affected by landforms. Their region has typical jobs and customs. For example, the fertile soil of the Mississippi lowlands helps farmers in the region grow crops.

4. Movement

Passenger train

Throughout history, people have moved to find better land or a better life. Geographers study why these *movements* occurred. They also study how people's movements have changed a region.

5. Human Interaction

Hoover Dam

Geographers study the ways that people adapt to their environment. Geographers also study how people change their environment. The *interaction* between people and their environment explains how land is used.

Dictionary of Geographic Terms

1 BASIN A bowl-shaped landform surrounded by higher land

2 BAY Part of an ocean or lake that extends deeply into the land

3 CANAL A channel built to carry water for irrigation or transportation

4 CANYON A deep, narrow valley with steep sides

5 COAST The land along an ocean

6 DAM A wall built across a river, creating a lake that stores water

7 DELTA Land made of soil left behind as a river drains into a larger body of water

8 DESERT A dry environment with few plants and animals

9 FAULT The border between two of the plates that make up Earth's crust

10 GLACIER A huge sheet of ice that moves slowly across the land

11 GULF Part of an ocean that extends into the land; larger than a bay

12 HARBOR A sheltered place along a coast where boats dock safely

13 HILL A rounded, raised landform; not as high as a mountain

14 ISLAND A body of land completely surrounded by water

15 LAKE A body of water completely surrounded by land

16 MESA A hill with a flat top; smaller than a plateau

17 **MOUNTAIN** A high landform with steep sides; higher than a hill

18 **MOUNTAIN PASS** A narrow gap through a mountain range

19 **MOUTH** The place where a river empties into a larger body of water

20 **OCEAN** A large body of salt water; oceans cover much of Earth's surface

21 **PENINSULA** A body of land nearly surrounded by water

22 **PLAIN** A large area of nearly flat land

23 **PLATEAU** A high, flat area that rises steeply above the surrounding land

24 **PORT** A place where ships load and unload their goods

25 **RESERVOIR** A natural or artificial lake used to store water

26 **RIVER** A large stream that empties into another body of water

27 **SOURCE** The starting point of a river

28 **VALLEY** An area of low land between hills or mountains

29 **VOLCANO** An opening in Earth's surface through which hot rock and ash are forced out

30 **WATERFALL** A flow of water falling vertically

Reviewing Geography Skills

Read a Map

Maps are drawings of places on Earth. Most maps have standard features to help you read the map. Some important information you get from a map is direction. The main directions are north, south, east, and west. These are called cardinal directions.

The areas between the cardinal directions are called intermediate directions. These are northeast, southeast, southwest, and northwest. You use these directions to describe one place in relation to another.

In what direction is Iowa from North Carolina?

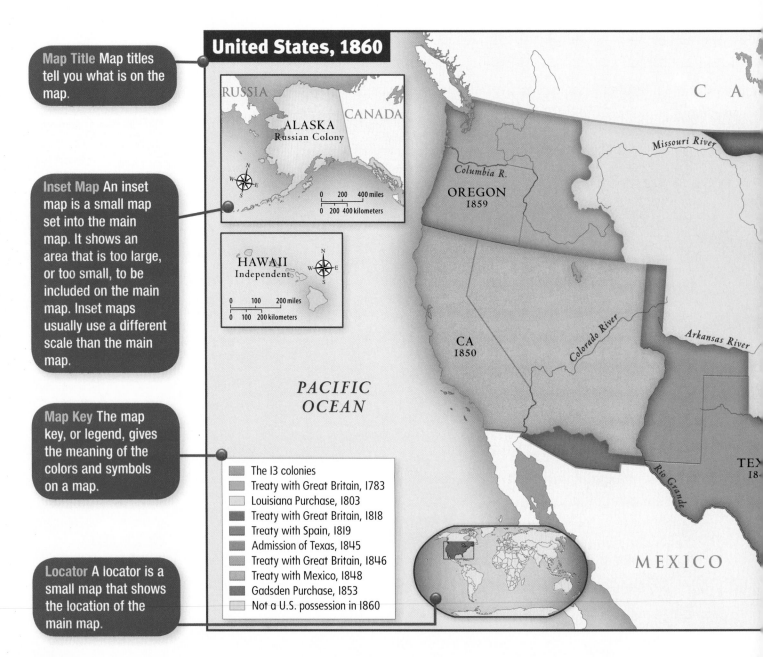

Map Title Map titles tell you what is on the map.

Inset Map An inset map is a small map set into the main map. It shows an area that is too large, or too small, to be included on the main map. Inset maps usually use a different scale than the main map.

Map Key The map key, or legend, gives the meaning of the colors and symbols on a map.

Locator A locator is a small map that shows the location of the main map.

United States, 1860

ALASKA
Russian Colony

RUSSIA

CANADA

0   200   400 miles
0   200   400 kilometers

HAWAII
Independent

0   100   200 miles
0   100   200 kilometers

PACIFIC OCEAN

OREGON
1859

Columbia R.

Missouri River

Colorado River

Arkansas River

CA
1850

Rio Grande

C A

TEX
18-

MEXICO

The 13 colonies
Treaty with Great Britain, 1783
Louisiana Purchase, 1803
Treaty with Great Britain, 1818
Treaty with Spain, 1819
Admission of Texas, 1845
Treaty with Great Britain, 1846
Treaty with Mexico, 1848
Gadsden Purchase, 1853
Not a U.S. possession in 1860

Read Historical Maps

Some maps capture a period in time. These are called historical maps. They show information about past events or places. For example, this map shows the United States in 1860 just before the beginning of the Civil War. Read the title and the key to understand the information on the map.

What year did California become a state?

Which states entered the Union after California?

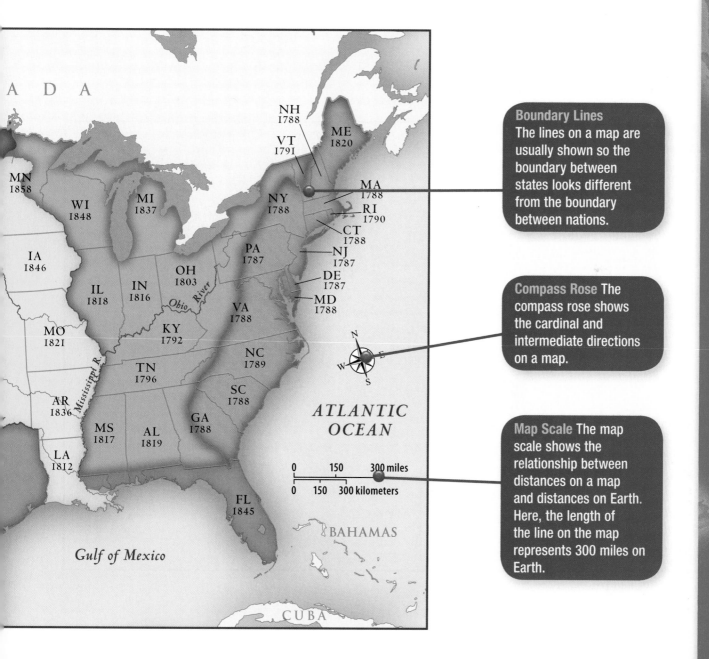

Boundary Lines The lines on a map are usually shown so the boundary between states looks different from the boundary between nations.

Compass Rose The compass rose shows the cardinal and intermediate directions on a map.

Map Scale The map scale shows the relationship between distances on a map and distances on Earth. Here, the length of the line on the map represents 300 miles on Earth.

Use Elevation Maps

An elevation map is a physical map that uses colors to show the elevation, or height of land above or below sea level. The height is usually measured in feet or meters. Sea level is measured as 0 feet or meters around the world. Read the key to understand what each color means. The map on this page uses purple to show land below sea level.

Identify the area of your town or city on the map. How high above sea level is your area?

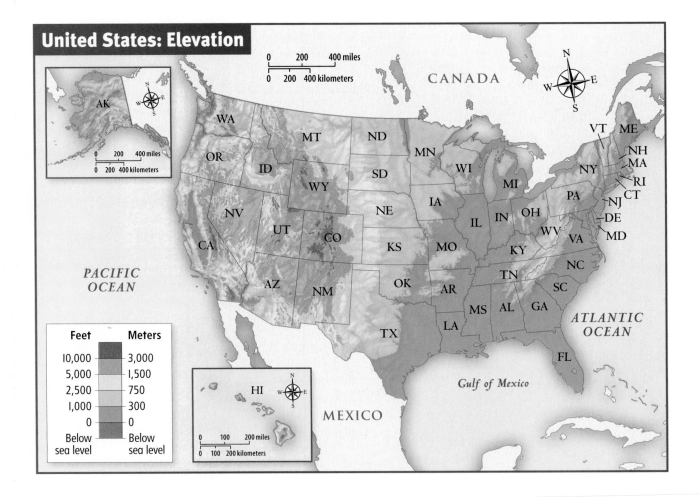

Use Road Maps

Suppose you want to go somewhere you have never been before. How do you know what road to take? You could use a road map. Road maps show where the roads in a certain area go. By reading a road map you can figure out how to get from one place to another.

Look at the road map of Indiana. The map key tells you which kinds of roads are shown on the map. Interstate highways run through two or more states and have two or more lanes in each direction. U.S. highways are usually two lane highways that also connect states. State highways stop at a state's borders. The name of each highway is a number. Notice the different symbols for each of the three kinds of highways.

Which roads would you use to get from South Bend to Terre Haute?

Hemispheres

The equator is an imaginary line on Earth. It divides the sphere of Earth in half. A word for half a sphere is *hemisphere*. The prefix "hemi" means half. Geographers divide Earth into four hemispheres.

All land and ocean north of the equator is in the Northern Hemisphere. All the land and ocean south of the equator is in the Southern Hemisphere.

Another imaginary line on Earth runs from the North Pole to the South Pole. It is called the prime meridian. It divides Earth into the Eastern Hemisphere and the Western Hemisphere.

Is North America in the Northern Hemisphere or Southern Hemisphere?

Is North America in the Eastern Hemisphere or the Western Hemisphere?

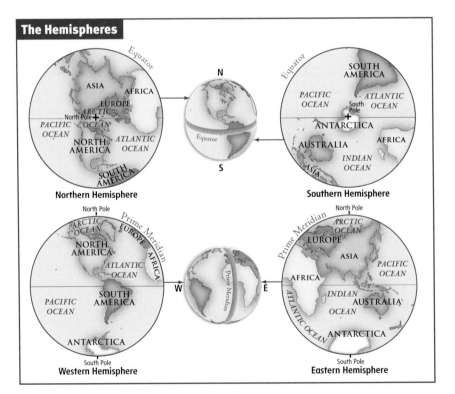

The Hemispheres

Northern Hemisphere

Southern Hemisphere

Western Hemisphere

Eastern Hemisphere

Earth-Sun Relationships

Earth revolves around the sun once a year. As it revolves, Earth also rotates on an axis. An axis is an imaginary line through the center of an object. Earth's axis is tilted 23.5° from due north. That tilt, plus the revolution of Earth around the sun, causes the seasons. The seasons are opposite in the Southern and Northern Hemispheres. For example, when it is winter in the Northern Hemisphere, it is summer in the Southern Hemisphere.

Latitude and Longitude

Geographers have created an imaginary system of lines on the Earth. These lines form a grid to help locate places on any part of the globe. Lines of latitude go from east to west. Lines of longitude go from north to south.

Lines of latitude are called parallels because they are an equal distance apart. The lines of latitude are numbered from 0 at the equator to 90 degrees (°) North at the North Pole and 90° South at the South Pole. Latitude lines usually have N or S to indicate the Northern or Southern Hemisphere.

Lines of longitude, or meridians, circle the Earth from pole to pole. These lines measure the distance from the Prime Meridian, at 0° longitude. Lines of longitude are not parallel. They usually have an E or a W next to the number to indicate the Eastern or Western Hemisphere.

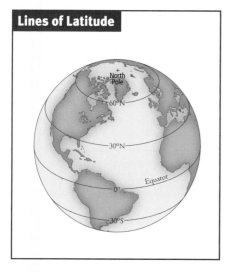

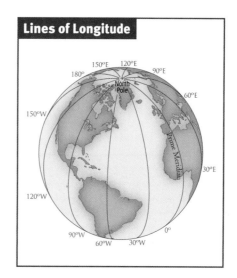

Absolute and Relative Location

You can locate any place on Earth using lines of latitude and longitude. Each line is identified by degrees (°). Each location has a unique number where one line of latitude intersects, or crosses, a line of longitude. This is called its absolute location. Each spot on Earth has an absolute location.

Relative location is the location of a place in relation to other landmarks. For example, St. Louis, Missouri, is located in eastern Missouri, along the Mississippi River.

> What is your absolute location? Use a map of the United States to find the latitude and longitude of the city or town where you live.

Maps at Different Scales

All maps are smaller than the real area that they show. To figure out the real distance between two places, most maps include a scale. The scale shows the relationship between distances on a map and real distances.

The scales on the maps in this book are drawn with two horizontal lines. The top line shows distances in miles. The bottom line shows distances in kilometers. You can use a ruler or mark a strip of paper under the scale to measure the distance between places on the map.

The maps on this page are drawn at different scales. Map A and Map B both show the Hawaiian Islands, but Map B shows a larger area with less detail. It is a small-scale map. Map A is a large-scale map. It shows a smaller area with more detail. The scales are different, but the distance between the places shown on both maps is the same.

On both maps, what is the distance in miles between Niihau and Molokai?

What details on Map A are not on Map B?

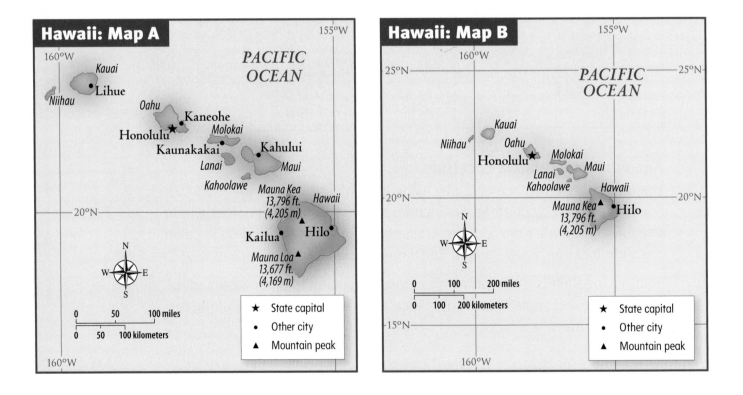

Use Population Maps

When you need to know the number of people who live in a place, or where people live, you can look at a population map. Most population maps show population density—how many people live in a certain area. Another kind of population map shows population distribution—where in an area people live.

Look at the population distribution map of the United States below. Population distribution maps often use different colors to stand for numbers of people per square mile or kilometer. The map key shows the number each color stands for. For example, between 5 and 24 people per square mile live in areas that are shaded yellow.

Which color is used to show the areas with the most people?

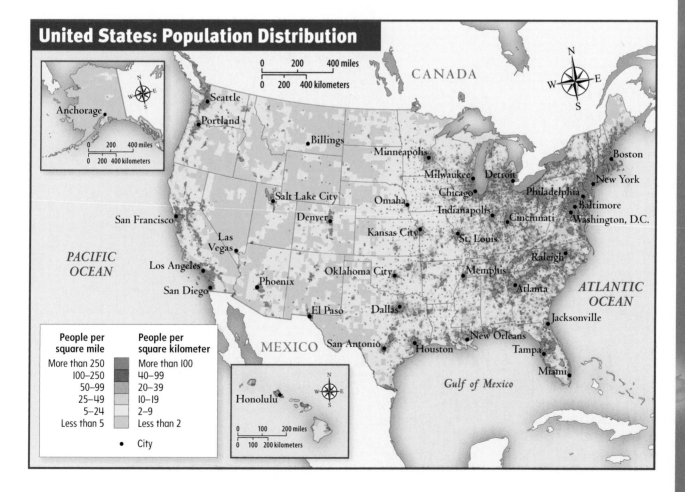

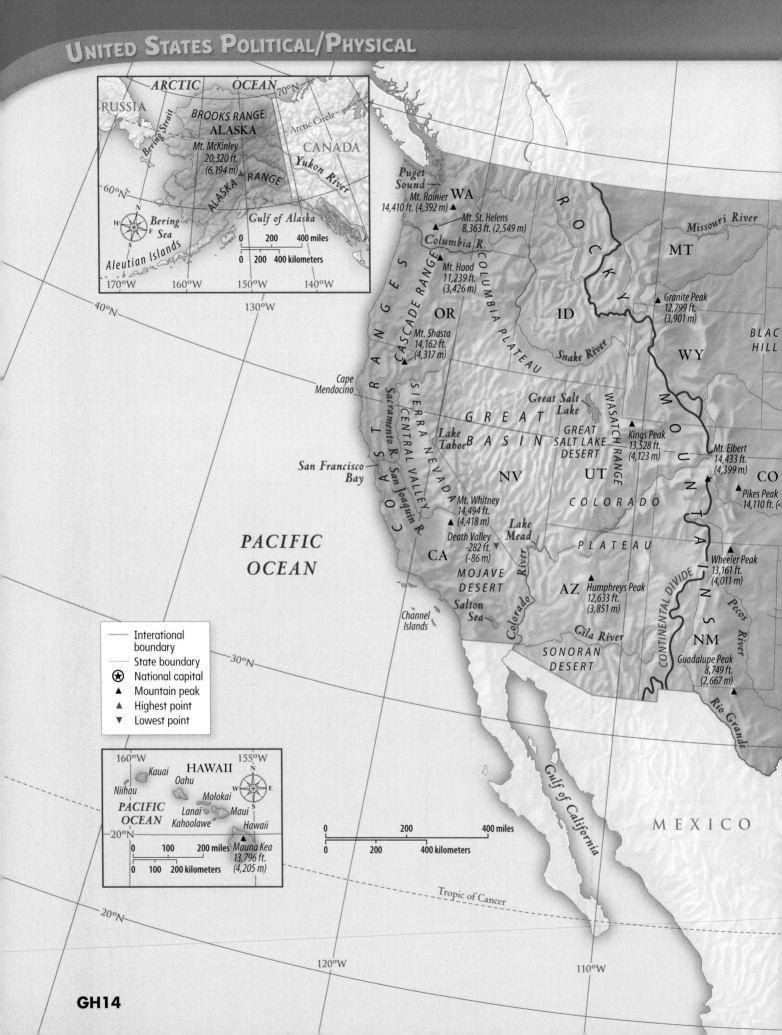

ARCTIC OCEAN
70°N
RUSSIA
BROOKS RANGE
ALASKA
Mt. McKinley
20,320 ft.
(6,194 m)
ALASKA RANGE
CANADA
Yukon River
Arctic Circle
60°N
Bering Sea
Gulf of Alaska
Aleutian Islands

N
W E
S

0   200   400 miles
0   200   400 kilometers

170°W   160°W   150°W   140°W
40°N
130°W

PACIFIC OCEAN

Cape Mendocino

San Francisco Bay

Puget Sound
Mt. Rainier
14,410 ft. (4,392 m) ▲
WA
Mt. St. Helens
8,363 ft. (2,549 m) ▲
Columbia R.
Mt. Hood
11,239 ft.
(3,426 m)
OR
Mt. Shasta
14,162 ft.
(4,317 m) ▲

CASCADE RANGE
COAST RANGES
SIERRA NEVADA
CENTRAL VALLEY
Sacramento R.
San Joaquin R.

COLUMBIA PLATEAU
Snake River
ID

ROCKY

Missouri River
MT

Granite Peak
12,799 ft.
(3,901 m) ▲

WY

BLACK HILL

Great Salt Lake
GREAT BASIN
GREAT SALT LAKE DESERT
WASATCH RANGE
Kings Peak
13,528 ft.
(4,123 m) ▲

Mt. Elbert
14,433 ft.
(4,399 m) ▲
CO
Pikes Peak
14,110 ft. (

Lake Tahoe
NV
UT
COLORADO
PLATEAU

Mt. Whitney
14,494 ft.
(4,418 m) ▲
Death Valley
-282 ft.
(-86 m) ▼
Lake Mead
CA
MOJAVE DESERT
Salton Sea
Channel Islands

Colorado River

Wheeler Peak
13,161 ft.
(4,011 m) ▲

AZ
Humphreys Peak
12,633 ft.
(3,851 m) ▲

Gila River
SONORAN DESERT

CONTINENTAL DIVIDE
MOUNTAINS

Pecos River
NM
Guadalupe Peak
8,749 ft.
(2,667 m) ▲

Rio Grande

PACIFIC OCEAN

30°N

International boundary
State boundary
⊛ National capital
▲ Mountain peak
▲ Highest point
▼ Lowest point

160°W   155°W
HAWAII
Kauai
Niihau
Oahu
Molokai
PACIFIC OCEAN
Lanai   Maui
Kahoolawe
Hawaii
20°N
Mauna Kea
13,796 ft.
(4,205 m) ▲

N
W E
S

0   100   200 miles
0   100   200 kilometers

0   200   400 miles
0   200   400 kilometers

Gulf of California

MEXICO

Tropic of Cancer

120°W   110°W
20°N

CANADA

Lake of the Woods

MESABI RANGE

Lake Superior

GREAT LAKES

St. Lawrence River

ME

ND

GREAT

MN

Mississippi River

Lake Huron

VT

Mt. Washington 6,288 ft. (1,917 m) ▲

GREEN MOUNTAINS

NH

SD

WI

MI

Lake Michigan

ADIRONDACK MOUNTAINS

NY

Lake Ontario

Hudson River

MA

RI

Cape Cod

CT

NE

IA

CENTRAL PLAINS

River

Lake Erie

ALLEGHENY PLATEAU

PA

Susquehanna River

40°N

NJ

Long Island

P

Platte

River

Missouri River

IL

OH

ALLEGHENY MOUNTAINS

River

MD DE

Delaware Bay

L

Wabash

IN

WV

★ Washington, D.C.

A

Ohio

River

River

Potomac River

Chesapeake Bay

I

KS

Arkansas

MO

KY

VA

Cape Hatteras

N

River

INTERIOR PLAINS

PIEDMONT

S

OZARK PLATEAU

TN

Tennessee River

Mt. Mitchell 6,684 ft. (2,037 m) ▲

NC

ATLANTIC OCEAN

OK

OUACHITA MOUNTAINS

Mississippi River

SC

ATLANTIC COASTAL PLAIN

Savannah River

Red River

AR

A P P A L A C H I A N   M O U N T A I N S

Brazos River

AL

River

GA

TX

Colorado River

MS

Alabama

Chattahoochee River

30°N

LA

EDWARDS PLATEAU

GULF COASTAL PLAIN

Mobile Bay

FL

Galveston Bay

Mississippi River Delta

Lake Okeechobee

BAHAMAS

Gulf of Mexico

Florida Keys

Straits of Florida

N

W ✦ E

S

CUBA

20°N

100°W

90°W

80°W

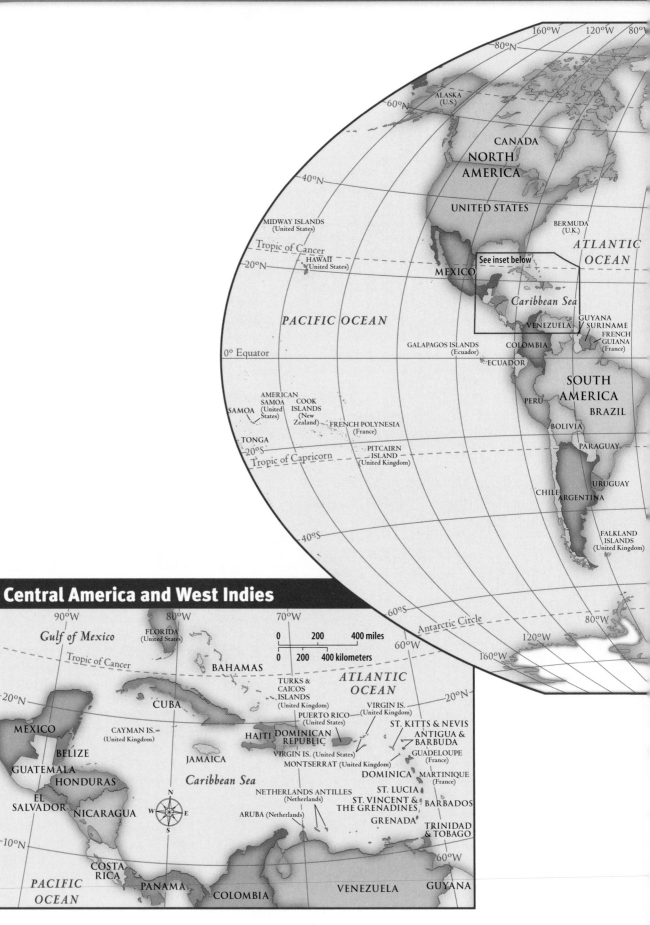

160°W 120°W 80°W

80°N

60°N

ALASKA (U.S.)

CANADA

NORTH AMERICA

40°N

UNITED STATES

MIDWAY ISLANDS (United States)

BERMUDA (U.K.)

ATLANTIC OCEAN

Tropic of Cancer

20°N

HAWAII (United States)

See inset below

MEXICO

Caribbean Sea

GUYANA SURINAME

VENEZUELA

FRENCH GUIANA (France)

PACIFIC OCEAN

GALAPAGOS ISLANDS (Ecuador)

COLOMBIA

0° Equator

ECUADOR

SOUTH AMERICA

AMERICAN SAMOA (United States)

COOK ISLANDS (New Zealand)

PERU

BRAZIL

SAMOA

FRENCH POLYNESIA (France)

BOLIVIA

TONGA

20°S

Tropic of Capricorn

PITCAIRN ISLAND (United Kingdom)

PARAGUAY

URUGUAY

CHILE ARGENTINA

40°S

FALKLAND ISLANDS (United Kingdom)

60°S

Antarctic Circle

60°W

80°W

120°W

160°W

Central America and West Indies

90°W 80°W 70°W

Gulf of Mexico

FLORIDA (United States)

0 200 400 miles

0 200 400 kilometers

ATLANTIC OCEAN

Tropic of Cancer

BAHAMAS

20°N

TURKS & CAICOS ISLANDS (United Kingdom)

VIRGIN IS. (United Kingdom)

20°N

CUBA

PUERTO RICO (United States)

ST. KITTS & NEVIS

MEXICO

CAYMAN IS. (United Kingdom)

HAITI DOMINICAN REPUBLIC

ANTIGUA & BARBUDA

BELIZE

JAMAICA

VIRGIN IS. (United States)

GUADELOUPE (France)

GUATEMALA

Caribbean Sea

MONTSERRAT (United Kingdom)

DOMINICA

MARTINIQUE (France)

HONDURAS

ST. LUCIA

EL SALVADOR NICARAGUA

NETHERLANDS ANTILLES (Netherlands)

ST. VINCENT & THE GRENADINES

BARBADOS

ARUBA (Netherlands)

GRENADA

TRINIDAD & TOBAGO

10°N

N W E S

60°W

COSTA RICA

PACIFIC OCEAN

PANAMA

COLOMBIA

VENEZUELA

GUYANA

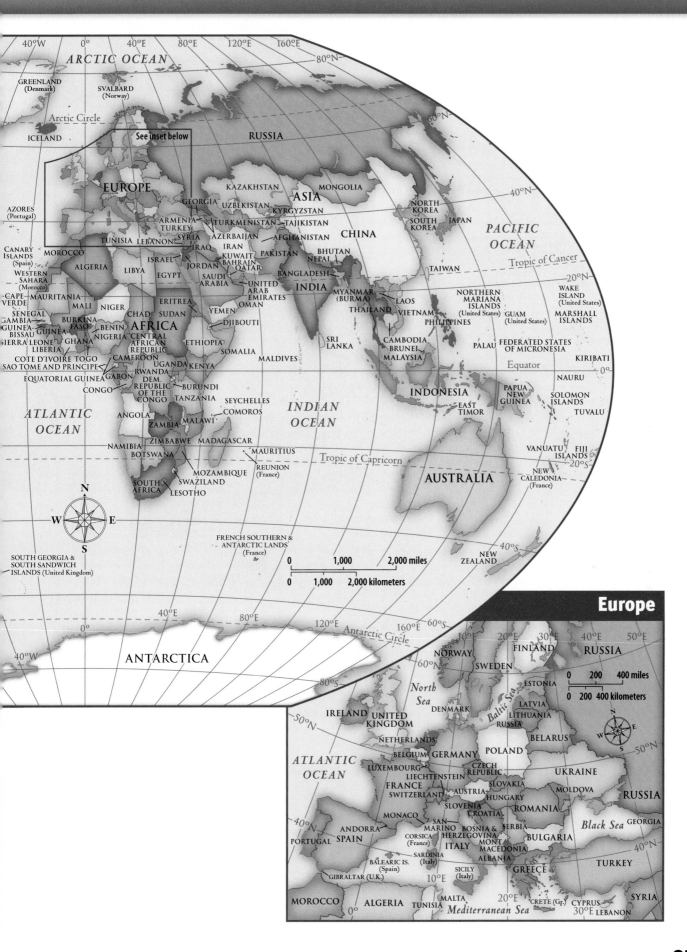

40°W   0°   40°E   80°E   120°E   160°E
ARCTIC OCEAN   80°N

GREENLAND   SVALBARD
(Denmark)   (Norway)
Arctic Circle
                              RUSSIA   60°N
ICELAND

EUROPE   KAZAKHSTAN   MONGOLIA
                    ASIA   40°N
AZORES   GEORGIA UZBEKISTAN NORTH
(Portugal)   ARMENIA KYRGYZSTAN KOREA JAPAN
              TURKEY TURKMENISTAN TAJIKISTAN SOUTH
TUNISIA LEBANON SYRIA AZERBAIJAN AFGHANISTAN CHINA KOREA PACIFIC
CANARY   IRAQ IRAN PAKISTAN BHUTAN   OCEAN
ISLANDS MOROCCO ISRAEL KUWAIT BAHRAIN NEPAL   TAIWAN   Tropic of Cancer
(Spain)   JORDAN QATAR BANGLADESH   20°N
WESTERN ALGERIA LIBYA EGYPT SAUDI UNITED INDIA MYANMAR   NORTHERN   WAKE
SAHARA   ARABIA ARAB EMIRATES (BURMA) LAOS   MARIANA   ISLAND
(Morocco)   OMAN   THAILAND VIETNAM   ISLANDS   (United States)
CAPE MAURITANIA   ERITREA YEMEN   (United States) GUAM MARSHALL
VERDE   MALI NIGER CHAD SUDAN   PHILIPPINES   (United States) ISLANDS
SENEGAL BURKINA   DJIBOUTI
GAMBIA FASO BENIN   ETHIOPIA SRI   CAMBODIA PALAU FEDERATED STATES
GUINEA- GUINEA NIGERIA CENTRAL   LANKA   BRUNEI   OF MICRONESIA KIRIBATI
BISSAU   AFRICAN   MALDIVES MALAYSIA
SIERRA LEONE GHANA REPUBLIC SOMALIA   Equator   0°
COTE D'IVOIRE TOGO CAMEROON UGANDA KENYA   NAURU
SAO TOME AND PRINCIPE   INDONESIA PAPUA SOLOMON
EQUATORIAL GUINEA GABON RWANDA BURUNDI   NEW   ISLANDS
CONGO DEM.   REPUBLIC TANZANIA SEYCHELLES INDIAN   EAST GUINEA TUVALU
ATLANTIC   OF THE CONGO   OCEAN   TIMOR
OCEAN   ANGOLA MALAWI COMOROS
            ZAMBIA   VANUATU FIJI
            ZIMBABWE MADAGASCAR   ISLANDS   20°S
NAMIBIA   MAURITIUS   Tropic of Capricorn
BOTSWANA   REUNION   NEW
        N   MOZAMBIQUE (France)   AUSTRALIA CALEDONIA
SOUTH SWAZILAND   (France)
W E AFRICA LESOTHO

    S
SOUTH GEORGIA &   FRENCH SOUTHERN &
SOUTH SANDWICH   ANTARCTIC LANDS   40°S
ISLANDS (United Kingdom)   (France)   NEW
                                                          ZEALAND

                        0   1,000   2,000 miles

                        0   1,000   2,000 kilometers

        40°E   80°E   120°E   160°E   60°S
                              Antarctic Circle
    0°   Europe
40°W   ANTARCTICA   80°S

                                        10°E 20°E 30°E 40°E 50°E
                                    NORWAY FINLAND RUSSIA
                                        60°N SWEDEN   0   200   400 miles
                                    North   ESTONIA 0 200 400 kilometers
                                    Sea   DENMARK   LATVIA
                                IRELAND UNITED   LITHUANIA
                                    KINGDOM   RUSSIA
                                        NETHERLANDS   BELARUS 50°N
                                ATLANTIC BELGIUM GERMANY POLAND
                                OCEAN LUXEMBOURG CZECH UKRAINE
                                    LIECHTENSTEIN REPUBLIC
                                    FRANCE SLOVAKIA
                                    SWITZERLAND AUSTRIA HUNGARY MOLDOVA RUSSIA
                                        SLOVENIA   ROMANIA
                                    MONACO   CROATIA
                                50°N SAN BOSNIA &   SERBIA Black Sea GEORGIA
                                40° ANDORRA MARINO HERZEGOVINA MONT. BULGARIA
                                PORTUGAL SPAIN CORSICA ITALY MACEDONIA   40°N
                                        (France)   ALBANIA GREECE TURKEY
                                        SARDINIA
                                    BALEARIC IS. (Italy)   SICILY
                                    (Spain)   (Italy)   SYRIA
                                    GIBRALTAR (U.K.) 10°E   GREECE CYPRUS LEBANON
                            MOROCCO ALGERIA TUNISIA MALTA CRETE (Gr.)
                                            20°E Mediterranean Sea 30°E

ARCTIC OCEAN

40°E 80°E 120°E 160°E
80°N

Lena River
Yenisey River
Ob River
URAL MTS.
Volga River
60°N

EUROPE
ALPS
Mont Blanc
15,711 ft.
(4,807 m)

Caspian Sea

ASIA

GOBI

Sea of Okhotsk

40°N

Black Sea   Mt. Elbrus
18,510 ft.
(5,642 m)

HINDU KUSH

Mediterranean Sea

SYRIAN
DESERT

SAHARA

Nile River

Red Sea

HIMALAYA

Mt. Everest
29,035 ft.
(8,850 m)

Yangtze River

Tropic of Cancer

20°N

Ganges River

DECCAN
PLATEAU

Arabian
Sea

South
China
Sea

Philippine
Sea

PACIFIC OCEAN

AFRICA

Congo River

Mt. Kilimanjaro
19,340 ft.
(5,895 m)

Equator   0°

INDIAN
OCEAN

NAMIB DESERT

KALAHARI
DESERT

Coral
Sea

Tropic of Capricorn

GREAT
SANDY
DESERT

20°S

AUSTRALIA

Cape of
Good Hope

Darling River

Mt. Kosciuszko
7,310 ft.
(2,228 m)

40°S

N
W   E
S

0   1,000   2,000 miles
0   1,000   2,000 kilometers

40°E   80°E   120°E   160°E   60°S

Antarctic Circle

80°S

ANTARCTICA

EUROPE

ASIA

ARCTIC OCEAN

Oodaaq Island

Lincoln Sea

Greenland Sea

Gunnbjorn 12,139 ft. (3,700 m)

ICELAND

Chukchi Sea

Point Barrow

Queen Elizabeth Islands

Ellesmere Island

HAYES PENINSULA

Bering Strait

Bering Sea

SEWARD PENINSULA

NORTH SLOPE

BROOKS RANGE

Beaufort Sea

Banks Island

Melville Island

Devon Island

Somerset Island

Prince of Wales I.

Greenland

Mt. McKinley 20,320 ft. (6,194 m) ▲ ALASKA

Yukon R.

ALASKA RANGE

YUKON PLATEAU

MACKENZIE MTS.

Mackenzie R.

Victoria Island

BOOTHIA PENINSULA MELVILLE PEN.

Baffin Island

Baffin Bay

Davis Strait

Arctic Circle

Cape Farewell

KENAI PENINSULA

▲ Mt. Logan 19,551 ft. (5,959 m)

Great Bear Lake

Foxe Basin

Labrador Sea

Kodiak Island

Gulf of Alaska

ALEXANDER ARCHIPELAGO

C A N A D A

Peace R.

Slave R.

Great Slave Lake

Southampton Island

Hudson Strait

Ungava Bay

COAST MOUNTAINS

ROCKY

COLUMBIA MTS.

Lake Athabasca

Churchill R.

Hudson Bay

Belcher Islands

Island of Newfoundland

Queen Charlotte Islands

FRASER PLATEAU

Saskatchewan R.

C A N A D I A N   S H I E L D

James Bay

LAURENTIAN MTS.

Gulf of St. Lawrence

AVALON PENINSULA

Cape Breton Island

Vancouver Island

OLYMPIC PENINSULA

CASCADE RANGE

COLUMBIA PLATEAU

Snake R.

Lake Winnipeg

Lake Superior

Lake Huron

GASPÉ PEN.

St. Lawrence

Nova Scotia

Prince Edward Island

COAST RANGES

SIERRA NEVADA

Great Salt Lake

GREAT BASIN

COLORADO PLATEAU

Missouri River

Ottawa ✪

Lake Michigan

Lake Ontario

Lake Erie

Gulf of Maine

Bay of Fundy

Cape Mendocino

MOUNTAINS

HIGH PLAINS

Platte R.

CENTRAL LOWLAND

Ohio R.

APPALACHIAN MOUNTAINS

Cape Cod

Long Island

ATLANTIC OCEAN

▲ Mt. Whitney 14,494 ft. (4,418 m)

U N I T E D   S T A T E S

Washington, D.C. ✪

Chesapeake Bay

Death Valley -282 ft. (-86 m)

Colorado

Grand Canyon

Arkansas River

OZARK PLATEAU

Mississippi R.

Cape Hatteras

Bermuda (U.K.)

Channel Islands

SONORAN DESERT

Red River

COASTAL

PACIFIC OCEAN

BAJA CALIFORNIA

Rio Grande

SIERRA MADRE OCCIDENTAL

Gulf of California

PLAIN

Tropic of Cancer

BAHAMAS

Nassau

DOMINICAN REPUBLIC

Gulf of Mexico

Florida Keys

W E S T   I N D I E S

Tropic of Cancer

M E X I C O

SIERRA MADRE ORIENTAL

Havana ✪

CUBA

Hispaniola

HAITI

Virgin Islands Guadeloupe

Orizaba 18,855 ft. (5,747 m) ▲

YUCATÁN PENINSULA

Cozumel Island

Cayman Islands (U.K.)

Port-au-Prince ✪

Kingston ✪

Santo Domingo ✪

Martinique

Puerto Rico (U.S.)

México City ✪

GUATEMALA

BELIZE

JAMAICA

TRINIDAD & TOBAGO

Belmopan ✪

Isthmus of Tehuantepec

HONDURAS

Caribbean Sea

Port-of-Spain ✪

Guatemala City ✪

Tegucigalpa ✪

San Salvador ✪

NICARAGUA

EL SALVADOR

Managua ✪

Lake Nicaragua

COSTA RICA

Isthmus of Panama

San José ✪

PANAMA

Panamá ✪

SOUTH AMERICA

CENTRAL AMERICA

Equator

Legend:
- International boundary
- ✪ National capital
- ▲ Mountain peak

N
W E
S

0   300   600 miles
0   300   600 kilometers

SOUTH AMERICA POLITICAL/PHYSICAL

NORTH AMERICA

ISTHMUS OF PANAMA

Caribbean Sea

N
W · E
S

Maracaibo
Caracas
VENEZUELA
Orinoco R.
GUIANA HIGHLANDS
Bogotá
Cali
COLOMBIA

GUYANA
Georgetown
Paramaribo
SURINAME
Cayenne
FRENCH GUIANA
(France)

ATLANTIC OCEAN

Negro River

Equator
Quito
ECUADOR
Guayaquil

Amazon River

AMAZON BASIN

River
Tapajos River
Xingú River
Tocantins River
São Francisco River

Galápagos Islands (Ecuador)

PERU
Lima
Arequipa

Madeira
River

ANDES MOUNTAINS

Lake Titicaca
La Paz
BOLIVIA
Santa Cruz
Sucre

BRAZIL

BRAZILIAN
Brasília
HIGHLANDS
River

15°S

ATACAMA DESERT

Mt. Ojos del Salado
22,572 ft.
(6,880 m)

Paraguay R.
PARAGUAY
Paraná

Rio de Janeiro
São Paulo
Tropic of Capricorn

CHILE

Mt. Aconcagua
22,834 ft. (6,960 m)

Asunción
River
Paraná

PACIFIC OCEAN

Valparaíso
Santiago
ARGENTINA
Concepción
PAMPAS

Rosario
Salto
URUGUAY
Montevideo
Buenos Aires
Rio de la Plata

30°S

PATAGONIA

ATLANTIC OCEAN

Falkland Islands
(Islas Malvinas)
(U.K.)

0   250   500 miles
0   250   500 kilometers

45°S

Strait of Magellan
TIERRA DEL FUEGO

South Georgia
(U.K.)

Cape Horn

— International boundary
⊛ National capital
• Other city
▲ Mountain peak

GH21

15°N
0°
15°S
30°S
45°S

105°W   90°W   75°W   60°W   45°W   30°W

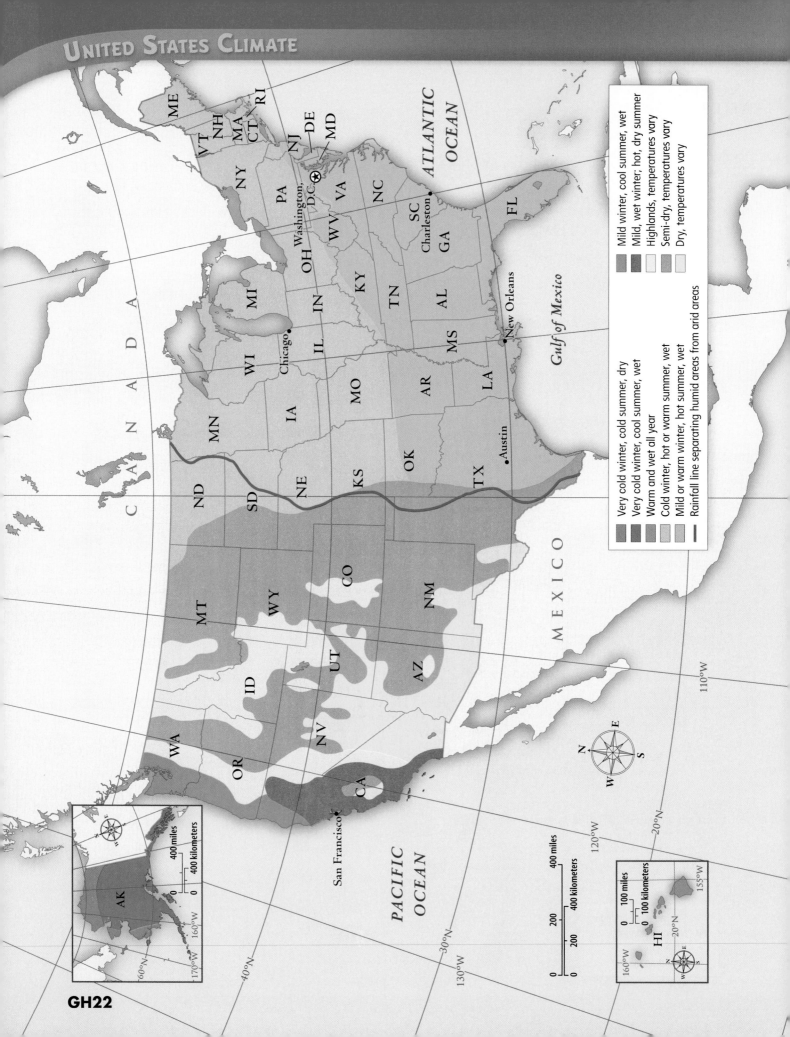

ATLANTIC
OCEAN

PACIFIC
OCEAN

Gulf of Mexico

CANADA

MEXICO

ME
VT NH
MA
CT RI
NY
NJ
DE
MD
PA
Washington, DC
OH WV VA
NC
IL IN KY
MI TN SC
WI Chicago SC Charleston
MO AL GA
IA AR MS
MN OK LA FL
SD NE KS New Orleans
ND
MT WY CO
NM Austin TX
ID UT AZ
NV
OR
WA
CA San Francisco

N
W E
S

160°W
170°W
60°N
40°N

AK

400 miles
0
0 400 kilometers

30°N

130°W

120°W

110°W

20°N

20°N

160°W
155°W

HI

100 miles
0
0 100 kilometers

400 miles
0
0 400 kilometers

200

200

N
W E
S

Very cold winter, cold summer, dry

Very cold winter, cool summer, wet

Warm and wet all year

Cold winter, hot or warm summer, wet

Mild or warm winter, hot summer, wet

Rainfall line separating humid areas from arid areas

Mild winter, cool summer, wet

Mild, wet winter; hot, dry summer

Highlands, temperatures vary

Semi-dry, temperatures vary

Dry, temperatures vary

Glossary

This Glossary will help you to pronounce and understand the meanings of the vocabulary terms in this book. The page number at the end of the definition tells you where the word first appears.

A

A.D. (ā dē) "Anno Domini." Latin for "in the year of the Lord." Used before a numeral to indicate a year occurring since the birth of Jesus Christ (p. 27)

abolitionist (ab ə lish'ə nist) a person who wanted to end slavery in the United States (p. 251)

absolute location (ab sə lüt' lō kā'shən) the exact location of a place expressed by longitude and latitude or street address (p. 59)

Adams-Onís Treaty (ad' əmz ō'nēs' trē'tē) Spain's agreement to sell Florida to the United States (p. 219)

adobe (a dō'bē) a type of clay traditionally used as a building material by Native Americans and, later, Spanish colonists in the Southwest (p. 24)

ally (a'lī) a person, group, or nation united with another in order to do something (p. 83)

amendment (ə mend'mənt) an addition to the Constitution. See **Constitution**. (p. 209)

ammunition (am ū nish'ən) objects, such as bullets, that can be fired from a weapon (p. 163)

Anaconda Plan (an ə kon'da plan) the Union's three-part plan for defeating the Confederacy and ending the Civil War (p. 262)

annex (ə neks') to make a country or territory part of another country (p. 313)

apprentice (ə pren' tis) a person learning a craft or trade from a master (p. 120)

archaeologists (är kē ol'ə jist) a scientist who looks for and studies artifacts. See **artifact** (p. 21)

arms race (ärmz rās) the effort build and acquire the most powerful weapons (p. 349)

arsenal (ar'sə nəl) a storage place for weapons (p. 198)

Articles of Confederation (är'ti kalz uv kən fed ə rā'shən) the first plan of government of the United States. It gave more power to the states than to the central government. See **Constitution** (p. 197)

artifact (är'ti fakt) an object made by humans long ago (p. 12)

assassination (ə sas ə nā 'shən) the murder of an important person (p. 278)

assembly (ə sem'blē) a lawmaking body (p. 137)

assembly line (ə sem' blē līn) a method of mass production in which the product is carried on a moving belt past workers (p.335)

B

B.C. (bē sē) Before Christ. Used after a numeral to indicate a year occurring before the birth of Jesus Christ (p. 27)

B.C.E. (bē sē ē) Before the Common Era. See **B.C.** (p. 27)

backcountry (bak kun'trē) Colonial area between the Appalachian Mountains and the Atlantic Coastal Plain (p. 122)

barter (bär' tər) the trading of goods for goods (p. 54)

battle map (bat'əl map) a map that shows the events of a conflict between two groups of armed forces (p. 177)

bill of rights (bil əv rīts) a formal statement of rights and liberties guaranteed to the people by a state. See **amendment** and **constitution** (p. 209)

black codes (blak kōdz) laws passed by the Southern states after the Civil War that severely limited the rights of the newly freed African Americans (p. 281)

blockade (blok ād') a barrier preventing the movement of troops and supplies (p. 187)

boycott (boi'kot) to refuse to do business or have contact with a person, group, company, country, or product (p. 157)

buffalo soldier (bəf ə 'lō sōl djər) an African-American soldier serving in the western United States after the Civil War (p. 314)

C

C.E. (sē ē) "Common Era" (p. 27)

cartogram (kär'tə gram) a map that shows information by changing the sizes of places (p. 311)

cash crop (kash krop) a crop that is grown to be sold for profit (p. 88)

cattle drive (kat' əl drīv) the movement of large herds of cattle, by cowboys, from ranches to the railroad (p. 293)

census (sen'səs) an official count of all the people living in a country or region (p. 6)

century (sen'chə rē) a period of 100 years (p. 27)

charter (chär'tər) an official document giving a person permission to do something, such as settle in an area (p. 87)

circa (sûr'kə) in approximately (p. 27)

circle graph (sûr'kəl graf) a kind of chart that shows how something can be divided into parts (p. 77)

citizen (sit'ə zən) A person born in a country or who legally becomes a member of that country (p. 9)

Civil Rights Act (siv'el rīts akt) a law that guarantees the individual rights of all citizens to be treated equally under the law (p. 354)

civil war (siv'əl wôr) an armed conflict between groups within one country. In the United States, the war between the Union and the Confederacy from 1861 to 1865 (p.257)

civilization (siv ə lə zā'shən) A culture that has developed complex systems of government, education, and religion. Civilizations usually have large populations with many people living in cities (p. 22)

clan (klan) a group of families who share the same ancestor (p. 44)

climate (klī'mit) the weather of an area over a number of years (pp. 4, 249)

climograph (klī'mō graf) a graph that shows information about the temperature and precipitation of a place over time (p. 249)

colony (kol'ə nē) a settlement far away from the country that rules it (p. 63)

Columbian Exchange (kə lum'bē ən eks chānj') the movement of people, plants, animals, and germs in either direction across the Atlantic Ocean following the voyages of Columbus (p. 64)

common (kom'ən) the village green or center of Puritan villages characterized by the presence of a Puritan church or meeting house (p. 102)

communism (kom'ū nism) the political system in which the government owns all property and distributes resources to its citizens (p. 347)

commute (kə 'myüt) to travel back and forth regularly (p. 307)

concentration camps (kon sen trā shun kamps) prisons where Nazis enslaved and murdered millions of people during WW II (p. 345)

conquistador (kon kēs'tə dôr) a name for the Spanish conquerors who first came to the Americas in the 1500s (p. 67)

Continental army (kon'tə nen'təl är'mē) the army created by the Second Continental Congress in May 1775 with George Washington as commander-in-chief (p. 149)

corporation (kôr pə rā'shən) a form of business in which holders of shares of stock are the owners of the business (p. 304)

cost-benefit decision (kost 'ben ə fit dis izh'ən) A choice made to buy a product taking into consideration the future benefits that will result from the product (p. 11)

cotton gin (kot'ən jin) a machine that separates cotton from its seeds, invented by Eli Whitney in 1793 (p. 223)

coup stick (kü stik) a weapon used by a Lakota Sioux fighter to show bravery by touching, but not killing, an enemy (p. 39)

coureurs de bois (kü rər' də bwä') in New France, a person who trapped furs without permission from the French government (p. 84)

covenant (ku' və nənt) a contract, an agreement (p. 102)

Creek Confederacy (krēk kən fed'ər ə sē) the union formed by several groups of Creek Indians to protect themselves (p. 44)

culture (kul'chər) the entire way of life of a people, including their customs, beliefs, and language (p. 12)

D

debate (dē bāt') a formal argument about different political ideas (p. 255)

debtor (det'ər) a person who owes money (p. 115)

Declaration of Independence (dek lə rā'shən əv in də pen'dəns) the official document issued on July 4, 1776, announcing that the American colonies were breaking away from Great Britain (p. 150)

delegate (del'ə git) a member of an elected assembly. See **assembly** (p.159)

demand (di mand') the desire for a product or service. See **supply** (p. 11)

desert (di'zərt) to go away and leave a person or thing that should not be left (p.179)

dictator (dik'tā tor) ruler or leader with absolute power (p. 341)

discrimination (di skrim ə nā'shən) an unfair difference in the treatment of people (p. 231)

draft (draft) the selecting of persons for military service or some other special duty (p. 259)

E

economy (i kon'ə mē) the way a country's people use natural resources, money, and knowledge to produce goods and services (p. 10)

ecosystem (ē'kō sis'təm) all the living and nonliving things in a certain area (p. 3)

Emancipation Proclamation (ē man si pā'shən prok lə mā'shən) the official announcement issued by President Abraham Lincoln in 1862 that led to the end of slavery in the United States (p. 267)

empire (em'pīr) an area in which different groups of people are controlled by one ruler or government (p. 67)

enslave (en slāv') to force a person to work for no money without the freedom to leave (p.75)

environment (en vī'rən mənt) all the surroundings in which people, plants, and animals live (p. 3)

Era of Good Feelings (îr'ə uv gǔd fē'lingz) the name given to the period of peace and prosperity that followed the War of 1812 (p. 219)

era (îr'ə) a period of time or history (p. 351)

ethnic group (eth'nik grüp) people who share the same customs and language, and often a common history (p. 7)

exoduster (ek'so dus tər) An African American from the South who went to Kansas in the 1870s (p. 297)

expedition (ek spi dish'ən) a journey made for a special purpose (p. 61)

export (ek'spôrt) to send goods to other countries for sale or use (p. 84)

F

federal system (fed'ər əl sis'təm) a system of government in which power in the nation is shared between the central government and the state governments (p. 205)

free state (frē stāt) state where slavery was banned (p. 246)

French and Indian War (french ənd in'dē ən wôr) a conflict between Great Britain and France in North America from 1756 to 1763 (p. 153)

frontier (frun tēr') the name given by colonists to the far end of a country where people are just beginning to settle (p. 73)

fundamental (fun də men'təl) something basic or necessary (p. 103)

G

Gettysburg Address (get'iz burg ə dres') a speech made by President Lincoln at the site of the Battle of Gettysburg in 1863 (p. 271)

glacier (glā' shər) a large mass of ice (p. 21)

global grid (glō'bəl grid) a set of squares formed by crisscrossing lines that can help you determine the absolute location of a place on a globe (p. 59)

global warming (glō' bəl wär' ming) the gradual increase of the Earth's temperature (p. 364)

Gold Rush (gōld rush) the sudden rush of people to an area where gold has been discovered (p. 236)

Great Awakening (grāt ə wā' kən ing) a religious movement of the 1700s (p. 121)

growth rate (grōth rāt) an increase or decrease of something expressed in percentage (p. 121)

H

historian (hi stōr'ē ən) a person who studies the past (p. 12)

historical map (his tôr'i kəl map) a map that shows information about the past or where past events took place (p.123)

hogan (hō'gən) a Navajo dwelling (p. 35)

homesteader (hōm' sted ər) a person who claimed land on the Great Plains under the Homestead Act of 1862 (p. 295)

House of Burgesses (hous uv bər'jis əz) the law-making body of colonial Virginia, established in Jamestown in 1619 (p. 89)

I

immigrant (im'ə grənt) a person who leaves one country to live in another (p. 6)

import (im'pôrt) to bring goods from another country for sale or use (p. 84)

impressment (im pres´mənt) the act of seizing for public use or service (p. 215)

indentured servant (in den'chərd sûr'vənt) a person who worked for someone in colonial America for a set time in exchange for the ocean voyage (p. 89)

indigo (in'di gō) a plant that is used to produce a blue dye. See **cash crop** (p. 114)

Industrial Revolution (in dəs'trē əl rev ə lü'shən) the change from making goods by hand at home to making them by machine in factories (p. 223)

industry (in' dəs trē) a branch of business, trade, or manufacturing (p. 134)

inflation (in flā' shən) a rise in the usual price of goods and services (p. 176)

interchangeable part (in tər chan'jə bəl part) parts of a product built to a standard size so that they can be easily replaced (p. 223)

interdependence (in'tər di pen'dəns) dependence on each other to meet needs and wants (p. 364)

internment (in tərn' mənt) the isolation and confinement of people during a war (p. 343)

Iroquois Confederacy (îr'ə kwä kən fed'ər ə sē) the union of the five major Iroquois peoples beginning about 1570 (p. 45)

irrigation (ir i gā'shən) a method of supplying dry land with water though a series of ditches or pipes (p. 24)

J

Jim Crow laws (jim krō lôz) laws passed by Southern states after Reconstruction that established segregation, or separation of the races. See **segregation** (p. 285)

L

labor union (lā'bər ūn'yən) a group of workers united to gain better wages and working conditions (p.305)

large-scale map (lärj skāl map) a map that shows a smaller area in greater detail (p. 177)

latitude (lat'i tüd) an imaginary line, or parallel, measuring distance north or south of the equator. See **parallel** (p. 59)

League of Nations (lēg əv nā'shuns) an organization formed in 1920 by the Allied Powers of WW I to prevent further wars (p. 330)

legislation (le jəs lā'shən) laws passed by a law-making body (p. 137)

legislature (lej'is lā' chər) a body of people that has the power to make or pass laws (p. 200)

line graph (līn graf) a kind of graph that shows changes over time (p. 77)

lodge (loj) a type of home made of logs, grasses, sticks, and soil, which Native Americans of the Plains used when living in their villages. See **teepee** (p. 37)

longhouse (lông'hous) a home shared by several related Iroquois families (p. 43)

longitude (lon'ji tüd) an imaginary line, or meridian, measuring distance east or west of the prime meridian. See **meridian** and **prime meridian** (p. 59)

loyalist (loi'ə list) a colonist who supported Great Britain in the American Revolution (p. 172)

M

malice (ma' ləs) to want to harm someone (p. 278)

manifest destiny (man'ə fest des'tə nē) belief in the early 1800s that the United States was to stretch west to the Pacific Ocean and south to the Rio Grande (p. 229)

map scale (map skāl) a line drawn on a map that uses a unit of measurement, such as an inch, to represent a real distance on Earth (p. 221)

mass production (mas prō duk' shun) making large quantities of an item in order to keep costs low (p. 335)

mercenary (mûr'sə nər ē) a soldier paid to fight for another country (p. 172)

merchant (mûr'chənt) a person who buys, sells, and trades goods for a profit (p. 54)

merchant company (mûr'chənt kum'pə nē) a group of merchants who share the cost and profits of a business (p. 80)

meridian (mə rid'ē ən) any line of longitude east or west of Earth's prime meridian. See **longitude** and **prime meridian** (p. 59)

mestizo (me stē'zō) a person of mixed Spanish and Indian heritage (p. 76)

Middle Passage (mid'əl pas'ij) the middle leg of the colonial trade route in which captive Africans were shipped to the West Indies. See **slave trade** and **triangular trade** (p. 133)

migrant farm worker (mī'grənt färm wûr'kər) a laborer who moves from one farm to another as the seasons change (p. 356)

migrate (mī'grāt) to move from one place to another (p. 34)

militia (mə lish'ə) a group of volunteers who fought in times of emergency during the colonial period and the American Revolution (p. 161)

missionary (mish'ə ner ē) a person who teaches his or her religion to those who have different beliefs (p. 75)

Missouri Compromise (mə zûr'ē kom'prə mīz) an agreement in 1820 that allowed Missouri and Maine to enter the Union and divided the Louisiana Territory into areas allowing slavery and areas outlawing slavery (p. 246)

monopoly (mə nop'ə lē) a company that controls an entire industry (p. 304)

Monroe Doctrine (mən rō dok'trin) a declaration of United States foreign policy made by President James Monroe in 1823 that opposed European colonization or interference in the Western Hemisphere (p. 220)

muckraker (muk rā'kər) a newspaper writer who points out the misbehavior of public figures (p. 325)

navigation (nav ə gā'shən) the science of determining a ship's location and direction (p. 57)

neutral (nü'trəl) not taking sides (p. 341)

North American Free Trade Agreement (nôrth ə mer'i kən frē trād ə grē'mənt) a treaty signed by the United States, Canada, and Mexico in 1992 that makes all of North America one trading area (p. 364)

Northwest Passage (nôrth'west pas'ij) a water route believed to flow through North America to Asia that European explorers searched for from the 1500s to the 1700s (p. 79)

opportunity cost (äp ôr tün'ə tē kost) the value of the second best choice when choosing between two things (p. 11)

parallel (par'ə lel) a line of latitude. See **latitude** (p. 59)

parallel time line (par'ə lel tīm'līn) two different sets of events on the same time line (p. 27)

Patriot (pā'trē ət) an American colonist who supported the fight for independence (p. 171)

patroon (pə trün') the name given to wealthy Dutch landowners who were given land to farm along the Hudson River by the Dutch West India Company in the 1600s (p. 107)

pilgrim (pil' grəm) a person who travels to a place for religious reasons (p. 90)

pioneer (pī ə nîr') a person who is among the first of nonnative people to settle a region (p. 213)

plantation (plan tā'shən) a large farm that often grows one cash crop (p. 114)

potlatch (pot'lach) a feast given by Native Americans of the northwest coast, in which the guests receive gifts (p. 31)

poverty (päv'ər tē) the condition of being poor (p. 297)

prejudice (pre'jə dis) a negative opinion formed beforehand or without proof (p. 355)

primary source (prī'mer ē sôrs) a firsthand account of an event or an artifact created during the period of history that is being studied. See **artifact** and **secondary source** (p. 12)

prime meridian (prīm mə rid'ē ən) the line of longitude labeled 0° longitude. Any place east of the prime meridian is labeled E. Any place west of it is labeled W. See **longitude** (p. 59)

Proclamation of 1763 (prok lə mā'shən) an official announcement by King George III of Great Britain that outlawed colonial settlement west of the Appalachian Mountains (p. 154)

profit (prof' it) the money made on goods that exceeds the cost of production. (p. 54)

profiteering (prof'it ēr ing) making excess profits from goods that are in short supply (p. 176)

progressive (prə gres'iv) making use of new and creative ideas for change (p. 325)

property rights (prä'pər tē rīts) the rights to own or use something (p. 299)

proprietor (prə prī'ə tər) a person who owns property or a business (p. 108)

ratify (rat'ə fi) to officially approve (p. 208)

ration (ra'shən) to control the distribution of supplies (p. 342)

reaper (rē'pər) a machine that cuts grain for harvesting (p. 224)

Reconstruction (rē kən struk'shən) the rebuilding of the South after the Civil War (p. 281)

reform (ri fôrm') a change to improve the lives of many people (p. 325)

region (rē'jən) a large area with common features that set it apart from other areas (p. 4)

relative location (rel ə tiv lō kā'shən) a place in relation to another (p. 59)

repeal (ri pēl') to cancel (p. 157)

reservation (re sər vā'shun) territories set aside for Native Americans (p. 299)

sachem (sā'chəm) an Iroquois chief or tribal leader (p. 92)

satellite (sat'ə līt) an object that circles a larger object such as a moon (p. 350)

secede (si sēd') to withdraw from the Union (p. 257)

secondary source (sek'ən der ē sôrs) an account of the past based on information from primary sources and written by someone who was not an eyewitness to those events. See **primary source** (p. 12)

segregation (seg ri gā'shən) separation of people based on race (p. 285)

sharecropping (shâr'krop ing) a system in which farmers rented land in return for crops (p. 282)

slash-and-burn (slash and bûrn) to cut and burn trees to clear land for farming (p. 41)

slave codes (slāv cōdz) rules made by colonial planters that controlled the lives of enslaved Africans (p. 125)

slave state (slāv stāt) state where slavery was allowed (p. 246)

slave trade (slāv trād) the business of buying and selling people (p. 119)

slavery (slā'və rē) the practice of treating people as property and forcing them to work (p. 104)

slum (slum) a rundown neighborhood (p. 308)

small-scale map (smôl skāl map) a map that shows a large area but not much detail. (p. 221)

Spanish-American War (span'ish ə mer'ikən wôr) the war between the United States and Spain in 1898 in which the United States gained control of Puerto Rico, Guam, and the Philippines (p. 315)

spiritual (spi' ri tū əl) the religious songs of enslaved Africans (p. 127)

Stamp Act (stamp akt) a law passed by the British requiring colonists to pay a tax on paper products (p. 157)

steam engine (stēm en'jin) an engine that is powered by compressed steam (p. 224)

stock (stok) a share in the ownership of a company (p. 337)

strike (strīk) a refusal of all the workers in a business to work until the owners meet their demands (p. 305)

suffrage (suf'rij) the right to vote (p. 333)

supply (sə plī') a quantity of something needed or ready for use. See **demand** (p. 11)

Supreme Court (sü prēm' kôrt) the head of the judicial branch of the federal government. It is the highest court in the country (p. 205)

T

tariff (tar' ef) a tax placed on imports or exports to control the sale price (p. 247)

tepee (tē'pē) a cone-shaped tent made from animal hides and wooden poles used by Native Americans of the Plains (p. 37)

tenement (ten'ə mənt) rundown building (p. 308)

territory (ter'i tôr ē) an area of land controlled by a nation (p. 149)

terrorism (ter'ər izm) the use of fear and violence by non-government groups against civilians to achieve political goals (p. 361)

time line (tīm' līn) a diagram showing the order in which events took place (p. 27)

time zone (tīm zōn) one of the 24 areas into which Earth is divided for measuring time (p. 331)

tolerate (tol'ə rāt) to allow people to have different beliefs from your own (p. 103)

total war (to' təl wôr) attacking an enemy's soldiers, civilians, and property (p. 264)

totem pole (tō təm pōl) a tree trunk that is carved with sacred images by Native Americans (p. 30)

Trail of Tears (trāl uv tîrz) the name given to the 800-mile forced march of 15,000 Cherokee in 1838 from their homes in Georgia to the Indian Territory (p. 229)

transcontinental railroad (trans kon ti nen'təl rāl'rōd) a railroad that crosses a continent (p. 294)

travois (trə voi') a kind of sled that is dragged to move supplies (p. 38)

treason (trē'zən) the act of betraying one's country (p. 256)

Treaty of Alliance (trē'tē əv ə lī'əns) the treaty signed between France and the United States during the American Revolution (p. 181)

Treaty of Guadalupe Hidalgo (trē'tē uv gwäd ə lü'pā ēdäl'gō) the treaty under which Mexico sold territory to the United States (p. 235)

Treaty of Paris 1763 (trē′tē uv par′əs) the agreement signed by Great Britain and France that brought an end to the French and Indian War (p. 154)

Treaty of Paris 1783 (trē′tē uv par′əs) The peace agreement in which Great Britain recognized the United States as an independent country (p. 187)

Treaty of Versailles (trē′tē əv vər sī′) the agreement that ended World War I (p. 330)

triangular trade (trī ang′gyə lər trād) three-sided trade routes over the Atlantic Ocean (p. 132)

tributary (trib′ yə ter ē) a river or stream that flows into a larger river (p. 149)

truce (trüs) an agreement to stop fighting that does not end a war (p. 349)

Union (yün′yən) states that are joined together as one political group (p. 277)

V

Voting Rights Act (vō′ting rīts akt) a 1965 law that guarantees U.S. citizens the right to vote (p. 355)

voyageur (vwä yä zhûr′) a trader who transported furs by canoe in New France (p. 84)

W

wagon train (wag′ ən trān) a group of covered wagons that follow one another closely to a destination (p. 229)

wampum (wom′pəm) polished beads made from shells strung or woven together used in gift-giving and trading by Native Americans (p. 43)

War Hawks (wôr hôks) members of Congress from the South and the West in the early 1800s who wanted the United States to go to war against Great Britain. See **War of 1812** (p. 217)

Index

*This index lists many topics that appear in the book, along with the pages on which they are found. Page numbers after a *c* refer you to a chart or diagram, after a *g*, to a graph, after an *m*, to a map, after a *p*, to a photograph or picture, and after a *q*, to a quotation.

Credits

Illustration Credits : 28: Yuan Lee. 42-43: Christian Hook. 45: Bill Farnsworth. 64-65: Bill Farnsworth. 99: (tr) Gary Overacre. 101: Dennis Lyall. 103: (tr) Steve Chorney. 118: Tom McNeely. 132-133: Roger Stewart. 152-153: Roger Stewart. 158-159: Chuck Carter. 196: Robert Papp. 240: John Kurtz. 264: Inklink. 294-295: (b) Frank Ricco

Photo Credits: All Photographs are by Macmillan/McGraw-Hill (MMH) except as noted below.

Volume 1: iv-v: David Stubbs/Getty Images. vi-vii: The Granger Collection, New York. viii: (bg) The Granger Collection, New York; (br) Victoria & Albert Museum, London/Art Resource, NY.

Volume 2: iv-v: Stock Montage/Hulton Archive/Getty Images. iv: Burstein Collection/CORBIS. v: The Granger Collection, New York. vii: Central Press/Hulton Archive/Getty Images. vi-vii: Jeff Hunter/Photographer's Choice/PunchStock.

1: Wesley Hitt/Mira.com. 2: (bl) Robert Holmes/Danita Delimont Stock Photography; (br) Radius/PunchStock. 2-3: (bg) David Stubbs/Getty Images. 3: Peter Griffith/Masterfile. 4-5: Dobbs Photography. 6: (bl) Bill Aron/PhotoEdit; (br) Robert Fried/Alamy Images. 6-7: (bg)Dirk Anschutz/Getty Images. 7: (bl) Michael Ventura/PhotoEdit; (br) CORBIS/PunchStock. 8: (b) Chris Clinton/Getty Images. 8-9: (bg) Eyewire/Punchstock. 9: (b) Mike Groll/The New York Times/Redux. 10-11: David R. Frazier PhotoLibrary. 12: Jeff Greenberg/The Image Works, Inc. 13: CORBIS/PunchStock. 14: Wesley Hitt/Mira.com. 16: (b) Hisham F Ibrahim/Getty Images; (t) stockbyte/PunchStock. 17: Taylor S Kennedy/Getty Images. 18: (bl) Kenneth Garrett/National Geographic Image Collection; (br) Marilyn Angel Wynn/Nativestock Pictures; (tl) National Anthropological Museum Mexico / Dagli Orti/Art Archive; (tr) Omni Photo Communications Inc./Index Stock Imagery. 19: (br) Artist Robert Griffing and his Publisher Paramount Press Inc; (tl) Pictures of Record, Inc.; (tr) Artist Robert Griffing and his Publisher Paramount Press Inc. 20: (bc) ML Sinibaldi/CORBIS; (bl) National Anthropological Museum Mexico/Dagli Orti/Art Archive; (br) Tom Bean/CORBIS. 20-21: National Anthropological Museum Mexico/Dagli Orti/Art Archive. 21: Kenneth Garrett/National Geographic Image Collection. 22-23: (bg) ML Sinibaldi/CORBIS. 23: John Elk III/Bruce Coleman Inc. 24: Tom Bean/CORBIS. 25: Joseph Froelich Collection/Ohio Historical Society. 26: National Anthropological Museum Mexico/Dagli Orti/Art Archive. 28: Lawrence Migdale Photography. 30: (l) Lawrence Migdale Photography; (r) Bob Daemmrich/PhotoEdit. 31: Rich Reid/National Geographic Image Collection. 32: (bl) Allen Russell/Index Stock Imagery; (br) Paul Conklin/PhotoEdit. 32-33: Chuck Place/Alamy Images. 33: (t) Allen Russell/Index Stock Imagery. 34: (inset) Paul Conklin/PhotoEdit. 34-35: (bg) Rob Crandall/The Image Works, Inc. 35: (c) Chuck Place/Alamy Images; (t) Marilyn Angel Wynn/Nativestock Pictures. 36: (bl) William J. Williams/National Geographic Image Collection; 36: Smithsonian Institution / Laurie Platt Winfrey/Art Archive. 36-37: William J. Williams/National Geographic Image Collection. 38: Courtesy, National Museum of the American Indian, Smithsonian Institution (21/8701). Photo by Ernest Amoroso. 39: (c) William J. Williams/National Geographic Image Collection; 39: Smithsonian Institution/Laurie Platt Winfrey/Art Archive. 40: (bl) Nathan Benn/CORBIS. 40-41: Nathan Benn/CORBIS. 45: Nathan Benn/CORBIS. 48: (b) Jules Frazier/Getty Images; (t) Photographer's Choice RF/PunchStock. 49: Private Collection, Index/Bridgeman Art Library. 50: (bl) MPI/Hulton Archive/Getty Images; (br) age fotostock/SuperStock; (tl) Michael S. Yamashita Photography; (tr) SuperStock. 51: (bl) Felipe Davalos/National Geographic Image Collection; (br) David Lyons/Alamy Images; (tl) The Art Archive/CORBIS; (tr) Paul Rezendes. 52: (bcl) Museo Real Academia de Bellas Artes, Madrid, Spain, Index/Bridgeman Art Library; (bcr) Frederiksborg Castle Denmark / Dagli Orti/Art Archive; (bl) The Granger Collection, New York; (br) John Farmar; Cordaiy Photo Library Ltd./CORBIS. 52-53: Scala/Art Resource, NY. 53: The Granger Collection, New York. 54: Museo Real Academia de Bellas Artes, Madrid, Spain, Index/Bridgeman Art Library. 55: Michael S. Yamashita Photography. 56: (c) Keren Su/CORBIS. 56-57: (b) Getty Images; 56-57: (t) Masterfile. 57: (tl) Frederiksborg Castle Denmark / Dagli Orti/Art Archive; (tr) The Granger Collection, New York. 58: (b) John Farmar; Cordaiy Photo Library Ltd./CORBIS; (t) Museo Real Academia de Bellas Artes, Madrid, Spain, Index/Bridgeman Art Library. 60: (bc) SuperStock; (bl) akg-images. 60-61: Ayuntamiento de Coruna, Spain/Bridgeman Art Library. 61: akg-images. 62-63: Steve Vaughn/Panoramic Images. 63: (b) akg-images; (t) SuperStock. 65: Steve Vaughn/Panoramic Images. 66: (c) T Bognar/Art Directors & TRIP Photo Library; (bl) H. Tom Hall/National Geographic Image Collection; (br) Victoria & Albert Museum, London/Art Resource, NY. 66-67: H. Tom Hall/National Geographic Image Collection. 68-69: T Bognar/Art Directors

& TRIP Photo Library. 70: Victoria & Albert Museum, London/Art Resource, NY. 71: (b) Werner Forman/Art Resource, NY; (c) H. Tom Hall/National Geographic Image Collection; (t) The Granger Collection, New York. 72: (bc) SuperStock. 72-73: The Granger Collection, New York. 73: The Granger Collection, New York. 74: SuperStock. 75: (bg) Massachusetts Historical Society; (br) Dick Davis, Ourmexico.com; (tl) Archivo de Indias, Seville, Spain, Mithra-Index/Bridgeman Art Library. 76: (bl) SuperStock. 78: (bl) The Granger Collection, New York; (br) Neil A. Meyerhoff Inc./Panoramic Images. 78-79: Erich Lessing/Art Resource, NY. 79: The Granger Collection, New York. 80: (t) The Granger Collection, New York. 80-81: (bg) Neil A. Meyerhoff Inc./Panoramic Images. 81: (c) Erich Lessing/Art Resource, NY. 82: (bl) Library and Archives Canada, Acc. No. 1990-329-5; 82: Private Collection, Archives Charmet/Bridgeman Art Library. 82-83: Painting: Jacques Cartier on Mount Royal, ca. 1933 © Library and Archives Canada. Reproduced with the permission of the Minister of Public Works and Government Services Canada (2006). Source: Library and Archives Canada/Lawrence R. Batchelor Collection/Accession 1983-45-6/C-010521. 83: (b) Library and Archives Canada, Acc. No. 1990-329-5. 85: (c) Painting: Jacques Cartier on Mount Royal, ca. 1933 © Library and Archives Canada. Reproduced with the permission of the Minister of Public Works and Government Services Canada (2006). Source: Library and Archives Canada/Lawrence R. Batchelor Collection/Accession 1983-45-6/C-010521; (t) Private Collection, Archives Charmet/Bridgeman Art Library. 86: (bcl) Richard T. Nowitz/CORBIS; (bcr) SuperStock; (bl) Transparencies, Inc.; (br) Bettmann/CORBIS. 86-87: Dean Cornwell/The Warwick New York Hotel. 87: Transparencies, Inc. 88: (inset) The Granger Collection, New York; (t) Richard T. Nowitz/CORBIS. 89: Joseph Martin/akg-images. 90-91: (bg) SuperStock. 91: (bl) Farrell Grehan/CORBIS; (c) Dirk Anschutz/Getty Images. 92-93: (b) Bettmann/CORBIS. 93: Dean Cornwell/The Warwick New York Hotel. 97: Collection of the New-York Historical Society, USA/Bridgeman Art Library. 98: (bl) James Hazelwood Photography; (br) The Granger Collection, New York; (tl) Bettmann/CORBIS; (tr) Shelburne Museum. 99: (bl) Margie Politzer/Lonely Planet Images; (br) Angelo Hornak/CORBIS; (tl) The Granger Collection, New York. 100: (bc) Bettmann/CORBIS; (br) The Granger Collection, New York. 100-101: William Owens/Alamy Images. 103: (b) Bettmann/CORBIS; (bg) Massachusetts Historical Society. 104: The Granger Collection, New York. 105: (c) The Board of Trustees of the Armouries/Heritage-Images/The Image Works, Inc.; (t) Mashantucket Pequot Museum, photo taken by Bob Halloran. 106: (bc) Culver Pictures/Art Archive; (bl) SuperStock; (br) Francis G. Mayer/CORBIS. 106-107: SuperStock. 107: The Granger Collection, New York. 108-109: Humanities and Social Sciences Library/Print Collection, Miriam and Ira D. Wallach Division of Art, Prints and Photographs/New York Public Library Picture Collection. 109: Culver Pictures/Art Archive. 110: Francis G. Mayer/CORBIS. 111: (c) Culver Pictures/Art Archive; (t) Hulton Archive/Getty Images. 112: (bl) Collection of the Maryland State Archives. Artist: Francis John Alfred Vinter (1828-1905), Title: George Calvert (1578/79-1632), Date: c. 1881, Medium: Oil on canvas, Dimensions: 62 x 43", Accession number: MSA SC 1545-1101. 112-113: Yale University Art Gallery, New Haven, CT, USA/Bridgeman Art Library. 113: Collection of the Maryland State Archives. Artist: Francis John Alfred Vinter (1828-1905), Title: George Calvert (1578/79-1632), Date: c. 1881, Medium: Oil on canvas, Dimensions: 62 x 43", Accession number: MSA SC 1545-1101. 115: Jane Faircloth/Transparencies, Inc. 116: Courtesy, Winterthur Museum. Gift of Henry Francis du Pont. 117: (c) Yale University Art Gallery, New Haven, CT, USA/Bridgeman Art Library; (t) Corpus Christi College, Oxford, UK/Bridgeman Art Library. 118: (bc) The Colonial Williamsburg Foundation; (br) The Granger Collection, New York. 119: Maritime Museum Kronborg Castle Denmark/Dagli Orti/Art Archive; (bl) Maritime Museum Kronborg Castle Denmark/Dagli Orti/Art Archive. 120: (bl) The Colonial Williamsburg Foundation; (br) Philadelphia Museum of Art/CORBIS. 121: Steve Gates/AP Images. 122: The Granger Collection, New York. 124: (bc) The Granger Collection, New York; (bl) SuperStock; (br) British Library. 124-125: Bettmann/CORBIS. 125: SuperStock. 126: The Colonial Williamsburg Foundation. 127: (b) The Colonial Williamsburg Foundation; (t) The Granger Collection, New York. 128-129: (bg) British Library. 129: (c) The Colonial Williamsburg Foundation; (t) Richard Cummins/CORBIS. 130: (bl) Private Collection/Bridgeman Art Library; (br) The Colonial Williamsburg Foundation. 130-131: The Colonial Williamsburg Foundation. 131: Private Collection/Bridgeman Art Library. 135: (c) Private Collection/Bridgeman Art Library; (t) The Colonial Williamsburg Foundation. 136: (bc) Historical Picture Archive/CORBIS; (bl) The Colonial Williamsburg Foundation; (br) The Granger Collection, New York. 136-137: The Colonial Williamsburg Foundation. 137: The Colonial Williamsburg Foundation. 138: Historical Picture Archive/CORBIS. 139: Michael Newman/PhotoEdit. 140: (inset) Atwater Kent Museum of Philadelphia, Courtesy of Historical Society of Pennsylvania Collection/Bridgeman Art Library. 140-141: (bg) The Granger Collection, New York. 141: (c) The Colonial Williamsburg Foundation;

290: (bl) Bill Manns/Art Archive; (br) Library of Congress, Prints & Photographs Division, John C. Grabill Collection, [LC-DIG-ppmsc-02527]; (tl) Bettmann/CORBIS; (tr) Bill Manns/Art Archive. 291: (bl) Dennis MacDonald/Alamy Images; (br) The Granger Collection, New York; (tl) Culver Pictures/Art Archive; (tr) The Granger Collection, New York. 292: (bl) Bettmann/CORBIS; (br) Bettmann/CORBIS. 292-293: SuperStock. 293: Bettmann/CORBIS. 295: Courtesy Central Pacific Railroad Photographic History Museum, © 2008, CPRR.org. 296: Bettmann/CORBIS. 297: (c) SuperStock; (t) Library of Congress, Prints & Photographs Division, Reproduction number [HABS KANS,33-NICO,1-7]. 298: (bl) Eastcott Momatiuk/Getty Images; (br) Christie's Images/CORBIS. 298-299: The Granger Collection, New York. 299: Eastcott Momatiuk/Getty Images. 300: (b) Christie's Images/CORBIS; (t) The Granger Collection, New York. 301: (c) Bettmann/CORBIS. 302: (bl) The Granger Collection, New York; (br) The Granger Collection, New York. 302-303: The Granger Collection, New York. 303: Photri-Microstock. 304: The Granger Collection, New York. 305: (l) Bettmann/CORBIS; (r) The Granger Collection, New York. 306: (bc) Hulton Archive/Getty Images; (bl) The Granger Collection, New York; (br) Jack Hollingsworth/Getty Images. 306-307: The Granger Collection, New York. 307: SuperStock. 308: R. Gates/Hulton Archive/Getty Images. 309: (b) Hulton Archive/Getty Images; (t) AP Photos. 310: (l) Jack Hollingsworth/Getty Images; (r) The Granger Collection, New York. 311: TBD Library of Congress, Prints & Photographs Division [LC-USZ62-98494]. 312: (bc) Collection of the New-York Historical Society, USA/Bridgeman Art Library; (bl) The Granger Collection, New York; (br) CORBIS. 312-313: The Granger Collection, New York. 313: The Granger Collection, New York. 314: (b) Collection of the New-York Historical Society, USA/Bridgeman Art Library; (inset) The Granger Collection, New York. 315: MPI/Hulton Archive/Getty Images. 317: (c) The Granger Collection, New York; (t) CORBIS. 318: Christie's Images/CORBIS. 320: David Roth/Getty Images. 321: Fred J. Maroon/Folio Inc. 322: (bl) age fotostock/SuperStock; (br) Bettmann/CORBIS; (tl) Peter Newark American Pictures, Private Collection/Bridgeman Art Library; (tr) Bettmann/CORBIS. 323: (bl) NASA/Time Life Pictures/Getty Images; (br) Jeff Hunter/Photographer's Choice/PunchStock; (tl) NASA/Getty Images; (tr) NewsCom. 324: (bcl) Hulton Archive/Getty Images; (bcr) The Granger Collection, New York; (bl) Underwood & Underwood/CORBIS; (br) The Granger Collection, New York. 324-325: The Granger Collection, New York. 325: (b) Alan Majchrowicz/Getty Images; (c) Underwood & Underwood/CORBIS. 326: (inset) Hulton Archive/Getty Images. 326-327: (bg) William Floyd Holdman/Index Stock Imagery. 328: (inset) Bettmann/CORBIS. 328-329: (bg) CORBIS. 329: (inset) The Granger Collection, New York. 330: (bl) Hulton Archive/Getty Images; (br) The Granger Collection, New York; (t) CORBIS. 332: (bcl) Hulton Archive/Getty Images; (bcr) Bettmann/CORBIS; (bl) From the original painting by Mort Kunstler, Suffragettes.©1987 Mort Kunstler, Inc. www.mkunstler.com; (br) Henryk T. Kaiser/Index Stock Imagery. 332-333: From the original painting by Mort Kunstler, Suffragettes. ©1987 Mort Kunstler, Inc. www.mkunstler.com.

333: Smithsonian American Art Museum, Washington, DC/Art Resource, NY. 334: (bg) Hulton Archive/Getty Images; (inset) Image courtesy of The Advertising Archives. 335: (l) Image courtesy of The Advertising Archives; (r) Art Archive. 336: (tl) Hulton Archive/Getty Images; (tr) FPG/Getty Images. 336-337: (bg) CORBIS. 337: (c) C Squared Studios/Getty Images; (t) Bettmann/CORBIS. 338: Henryk T. Kaiser/Index Stock Imagery. 339: (c) Hulton Archive/Getty Images. 340: (bc) Eliot Elisofon/Time & Life Pictures/Getty Images; (bl) The Granger Collection, New York; (br) AP Photos. 340-341: The Granger Collection, New York. 341: The Granger Collection, New York. 342: The Granger Collection, New York. 343: (b) Eliot Elisofon/Time & Life Pictures/Getty Images; (c) Cleve Bryant/PhotoEdit. 344: Bettmann/CORBIS. 345: (b) AP Photos; (t) The Granger Collection, New York. 346: (bc) CORBIS; (bl) Department Of Energy (DOE)/Time Life Pictures/Getty Images; (br) NASA/Getty Images. 346-347: Department Of Energy (DOE)/Time Life Pictures/Getty Images. 347: Keystone/Hulton Archive/Getty Images. 348: CORBIS. 349: Hulton Archive/Getty Images. 350: (b) Bettmann/CORBIS; (cr) The Granger Collection, New York. 351: (c) Department Of Energy (DOE)/Time Life Pictures/Getty Images; (t) NASA/Getty Images. 352: (bcl) AP Photos; (bcr) Dennis Cook/AP Photos; (bl) AP Photos; (br) Lionel Cironneau/AP Photos. 352-353: AP Photos. 353: Hank Walker/Time Life Pictures/Getty Images. 354: AP Photos. 355: (bl) Bettmann/CORBIS; (br) Central Press/Hulton Archive/Getty Images; (t) Vernon Merritt III/Time Life Pictures/Getty Images. 356: (l) Paul Fusco/Magnum Photos; (r) Dennis Cook/AP Photos. 356-357: (bg) Jason Reed/Reuters/Landov. 357: (l) Wally McNamee/CORBIS; (r) Barry Thumma/AP Photos. 358-359 (t): Hot Ideas/Index Stock Imagery. 358: (c) AP Photos; (l) Bob Daughtery/AP Photos; (r) Dirck Halstead/Time Life Pictures/Getty Images. 359: (c) Jason Reed/Reuters/Landov; (tc) J. Scott Applewhite/AP Images; (tl) Lionel Cironneau/AP Photos; (tr) Don Emmert/AFP/Getty Images. 360: (bc) Todd Pitman/AP Photos; (bl) Spencer Platt/Getty Images; (br) Eric Gay/AP Photos. 360-361: Spencer Platt/Getty Images.

361: Reuters/CORBIS. 362-363: Todd Pitman/AP Photos. 363: Thaier Al-Sudani/Reuters/Landov. 364: Eric Gay/AP Photos. 365: (c) Todd Pitman/AP Photos; (t) Brand X Pictures/PunchStock. 366: C Squared Studios/Getty Images. 368: (b) Digital Vision/PunchStock; (t) Tony Freeman/PhotoEdit

ACKNOWLEDGMENTS

Grateful acknowledgment is given to the following authors and publishers. Every effort has been made to trace the ownership of all copyrighted material and to secure the necessary permissions to reprint these selections. In the case of some selections for which acknowledgment is not given, extensive research has failed to locate the copyright holders.